MISSION AND MINISTRY
IN THE GLOBAL CHURCH

MISSION AND MINISTRY IN THE GLOBAL CHURCH

Anthony Bellagamba

ORBIS BOOKS

Maryknoll, New York 10545

The Catholic Foreign Mission Society of America (Maryknoll) recruits and trains people for overseas missionary service. Through Orbis Books, Maryknoll aims to foster the international dialogue that is essential to mission. The books published, however, reflect the opinions of their authors and are not meant to represent the official position of the society.

Library of Congress Cataloging-in-Publication Data

Bellagamba, Anthony.
    Mission and ministry in the global church / Anthony Bellagamba.
      p. cm.
    Includes bibliographical references.
    ISBN 0-88344-813-0 (pbk.)
    1. Catholic Church—Missions.   2. Missions—Theory.—I. Title.
BV2180.B455 1992
266'.2—dc20   92-19820
                                                CIP

TABLE OF CONTENTS

v

PREFACE

For thirteen years I worked at the United States Catholic Mission Council (which became in 1981 the U.S. Catholic Mission Association), a national office for the coordination and motivation of missionary efforts of the U.S. church. During that time I was privileged to visit U.S. missioners on all the continents. In my conversations with these dedicated men and women, I noticed they were preoccupied with some basic issues regarding mission and missionary activities. The same questions seemed to emerge in every conversation:

- What is mission today?
- What are the trends in society and in the church that affect it, challenge and shape it?
- Why do missioners who belong to the same church, and even to the same institute, exercise mission in so many different ways?
- What type of church do missioners operate out of? What type of church should they promote with mission?
- Should they promote church or mission?
- What type of spirituality do they need to help them grow as disciples, as cross-cultural ministers, and at the same time sustain them in the hardships of their ministries?

These and similar questions disturbed some missioners, challenged others, and opened new vistas—became life-giving—for many.

By listening to them, and being questioned by them, I was stimulated to review my own understanding of mission, of church, of ministry, to rethink many of my assumptions about spirituality and preparation for missioners.

As I was reformulating my own ideas about these topics, I would offer them to missioners in my conferences or retreats, or just in my conversations with them. Participation in national and international conferences, seminars, mission congresses, as well as extensive readings done on the same subjects, gave me the chance to challenge my insights, or to expand them, and confirm them.

This book contains the outcome of my intellectual and experiential journey in company with other missioners and colleagues the world over. It was written with the pastoral intent of helping cross-cultural personnel rethink their own mission, ministry, and the style of their presence in the world.

Though primarily addressed to persons who minister outside their own culture and country, I hope this book will be helpful to those who remain in their own countries, because cross-cultural situations are present every-where, and they will increase even more in coming years.

I wish to thank missionaries and colleagues who have helped me reshape my own perception of mission, church, ministry, and missionary spirituality. I thank the poor, especially those of Central and South America, who have given me a new vision and shared with me a new spirit. Special thanks go to Sr. Christiana Sestero, a Consolata sister, who corrected the manuscript, and to Dr. L. Namwara, editor of *African Christian Studies,* who has allowed me to use materials published in that journal.

I hope that all those who minister in cross-cultural situations, whether at home or abroad, will always be open to the Spirit of the Lord, to the signs of God's times, and will allow themselves to be challenged and inspired by the example of Jesus, of his mother, and of the many poor in the world. I pray that they will be courageous in continually renewing their mission, in faithfulness to the gospel and to the needs of the people.

ABBREVIATIONS

A.G.   *Ad Gentes*, Vatican Council II Decree on the Missions (1965).

C.D.   *Christus Dominus*, Vatican Council II Decree on the Pastoral Office of Bishops in the Church (1965).

D.V.   *Dei Verbum*, Vatican Council II Constitution on Revelation (1965).

E.N.   *Evangelii Nuntiandi*, Apostolic Exhortation on Evangelization in the Modern World, Pope Paul VI (1975).

G.S.   *Gaudium et Spes*, Vatican Council II Pastoral Constitution on the Church (1965).

L.G.   *Lumen Gentium*, Vatican Council II Dogmatic Constitution on the Church (1964).

P.O.   *Presbyterorum Ordinis*, Vatican Council II Decree on the Life and Ministry of Priests (1965).

R.H.   *Redemptor Hominis*, Encyclical Letter of Pope John Paul II (1979).

R.M.   *Redemptoris Missio*, Encyclical Letter of Pope John Paul II on the Missions (1991).

S.C.   *Sacrosanctum Concilium*, Vatican Council II Constitution on the Sacred Liturgy (1963).

S.R.S.   *Sollicitudo Rei Socialis*, Encyclical Letter of Pope John Paul II on Social Concern (1987).

1

MEGATRENDS AFFECTING THE CHURCH AND ITS MISSION

The historical context in which the church finds itself has become very important for the study of its own life, its activities and its theology. No one can attempt to do any serious reflections on the church and its mission in the world without taking it into account. The pope recognizes this when he states in *Redemptoris Missio:* "The rapid and profound transformations which characterize today's world, especially in the southern hemisphere, are having a powerful effect on the overall missionary picture" (37).

This context can be viewed from a particular background, or a national, continental, international, and even global background. Depending on the specific background one chooses, the reflections can be relevant to a church in a particular situation, or in a nation, a continent, and the whole world.

In this book, and more so in this first chapter, I will choose primarily, if not exclusively, the global context, with its megatrends, and see what kind of influence it has on the church, its mission, and what type of cross-cultural personnel would better serve that mission, how they should organize their ministries, and what type of formation and spirituality they would have to develop, in order to be faithful to the gospel and relevant to the world within its global context.

In this first chapter I shall briefly describe some megatrends which seem relevant to the church's mission, what kind of response they would require of the church, and what characteristics they would demand of cross-cultural personnel.

MEGATRENDS AND THE CHURCH'S RESPONSE

My first task is to offer an understanding of these megatrends as they relate to our subject. The megatrends I refer to here are those global trends which relate directly to mission, that affect mission, or say something special

1

to it, that call the church and its disciples to a different understanding of mission, or to different ways of carrying out its missionary work. Of course, these are not the only megatrends in the world. They are, however, the ones that have a direct influence on the mission of the church in the world.

Resurgence of Cultural Traditions

The first megatrend that has a bearing upon all the others, and will deeply affect the mission of the church in the world, is the resurgence among all the peoples of the world of a sense of their own cultural identity. This phenomenon is present in every continent and is manifested in a return to the roots of culture, to the original and living traditions, customs, under-standings, values, and relationships—a return not for its own sake, but for the sake of rediscovering identity, in order to cope with the modern world in ways that differ from one culture to another. This resurgence is present among native Americans of the U.S.A. and Canada, among all the tribes of Africa, among the tribal peoples of Australia and New Zealand, and among the black Americans, Chicanos, and Filipinos. This resurgence may eventually give way to multiculturalism, which means, according to a Cana-dian government ministry, that "people of diverse origins and communities are free to preserve and enhance their cultural heritage, while participating as equal partners in . . . society."

The reason for this movement was given a few years ago by Pope John Paul II when he declared in 1982 in Geneva:

It is above all in culture that man's essential resources are manifested. As I said at UNESCO, man lives a truly human life thanks to culture . . . Culture is that through which man as man becomes more man, is more, enters more into being . . . So culture thus becomes the foun-dation of man's ability to discover and utilize all his resources.

The response to this megatrend in mission is *inculturation*. In fact, incul-turation is a process by which the gospel enters into a culture, takes from the culture all that is already gospelled, and is enriched by it—the culture. In addition to this, the gospel challenges the culture in those aspects that are ungospelled and the culture challenges the gospel in those aspects which are merely Western, and thus both are purified and universalized. So the dynamics between culture and gospel are such that each is enriched and challenged by the other. There is a call and a response. And there is a rejection of elements of the culture which are contrary to the gospel, and a critique of and removal from the church of elements which are not the genuine gospel, but its westernized interpretation. Inculturation is a response to an exaggerated culturalism. And mission, with all its activities, should be marked by energetic commitment to inculturation. If it remains alien to a host culture, the church will at best be irrelevant to the people or even be rejected altogether.

Revival of Religious Experience

The second megatrend is the "religious revival" or, better, the revival of religious experience. People are thirsting for the divine, people are in search of the absolute, people are longing for personal religious experience. In India, Hinduism is growing stronger. In China, all the religions that took deeper roots in the lives and hearts of the people during the underground period have exploded into tremendous expressions of religiosity, with the advent of limited freedom. In North America and in the Western countries, the search for religious experience has reawakened in the young and the old. Today, religions and religious experiences are important in people's lives. The churches, the synagogues, the temples, all the structured religions of today, will have an influence on the lives of the people insofar as they provide opportunity for genuine religious experience. They will be judged unimportant as they become obstacles to this experience.

If the felt need for religious experience is a megatrend in the world, then, in the church's mission to the world, *dialogue* is the response that is needed at present. To make direct conversion the chief object of mission among peoples who are searching, under the influence of the Spirit, to kindle their own faith, deepen their own religiosity, may be an anachronistic attempt, perhaps even contrary to the movement of the Spirit. There is certainly a place for direct proselytism, direct conversion in every soul whom the Spirit may choose from among the people. These will gladly follow the Lord Jesus. But one of the major objects of mission may very well be dialogue among religions, rather than proselytism.

Basic Ecclesial Communities

The third megatrend affecting the church's mission is the need for personal encounter with God within the small faith communities. This may be a consequence of the other megatrend, the revival of religion, or it may be a particular development of it. The revival of religion can take place either as a mass phenomenon or as a personal encounter. At present, it often seems that the latter is more common. Both among Christians and among disciples of other religions, people come to God in small groups. Within the support and encouragement of a small group, people find their way to God, and God finds a way to the people. People long to experience God, to relate to God, to share their own faith with others in freedom and spontaneity, in an atmosphere of confidence and trust. They do not wish to be told that they are not qualified to speak about God because they have not studied theology, or are illiterate, or unacquainted with the latest human knowledge. They wish to share their religious experiences with one another, in freedom and without fear (O'Halloran 1991).

If that is a megatrend, then the *development of small faith communities* is the answer in today's mission. While in the past, the basic unit of the church may have been the parish, or a similar entity, at present the basic unit is the small faith community, at least in many areas of the world. It is there that the faith grows, freedom of the children of God is exercised, members enrich one another, and call forth in one another the gifts given to them by the Spirit. The small faith community is today's response to the individual's quest for God, and to personal and meaningful involvement for the transformation of humanity.

Problems in Ministerial Structure

The fourth megatrend affecting the church's mission is the inadequacy of the present way of ministry to respond to the needs of the people. This is especially true of the Catholic Church. Today in the church, people are thirsting for God; they long for the experience of God in their lives, and for participation in the life and ministry of the Catholic community. For this, they need help. It is true that the Spirit is ever-present, calling people to an intimate relationship with God, and to commitment to God's work for the building up of the kingdom. But, except in extraordinary circumstances, God makes use of the ministry of the church to help these people. To foster the development of spiritual life, there is the need to confirm, to direct, at times even to correct, and that can be done only through the loving ministry of Christ's church. But since at present, most of the ministries in the Catholic Church are entrusted to the priest — male, celibate, ordained — it is next to impossible for that one person to respond to the longings of the people of God for religious experience, and for personal involvement, and, in many instances, their quest for help cannot be answered (Power 1980, 12-37).

At present, the Catholic Church has approximately four hundred thousand ordained priests. According to a 1989 Vatican report on the distribution of priests, sixty-eight percent of these priests are in Europe and North America, where forty percent of the total church membership live. A mere twenty-two percent of ordained priests are scattered in the other four continents, where sixty percent of the world's Catholics live. It is almost impossible to meet the spiritual needs of our members, because of the way that ministry is presently structured in the church. And beyond the spiritual needs, what about all the other needs? What of the need for furthering development, social advancement, cultural identity? What of the needs of the poor and the oppressed, of those who are hungry and homeless, of refugees and the marginalized of society? The present structure of ministry in the church makes it impossible to respond adequately to the most essential needs of our adherents, let alone the needs of others.

If the present difficulties highlight a megatrend, then the response in mission is the *development of new and different ministries,* and of a *new style of ministry.* There is no reason why a given locality should depend on the ministry of one person. In that same locality, there may be others who have been called by the Spirit, and gifted with special charisms for the community, who must be brought into ministry, be they lay or religious, single or married, young or old, uneducated or professionals, male or female. The greater number of Catholics in Asia and Africa received their faith as the fruit of the devoted work of the local catechist, the lay leader of the community. In many places, the catechist could be called the founder of the local church, the leader of the community, the person who has fostered a growing awareness of God in the community, a love for God, and a concrete expression of that love of God in the commitment of the members to the good of the community.

The Western Church in Crisis

The fifth megatrend is the crisis in the Western church as an institution. The Western Catholic Church is in crisis, and it is in crisis because it is Western, because it has modified the universality of its nature and defined it in terms that may have been relevant to Westerners in the past but are irrelevant to them at present, and even more irrelevant to non-Westerners. The European and North American bishops attending the synods in Rome have had one major complaint to make: their churches are empty, they are abandoned, people do not go to church, and do not practice their faith any longer. This complaint was voiced especially at the synod on evangelization, on Christian education, and on the family. Because it has become identified with an antiquated form of Western culture and expresses the mysteries of God, of Jesus, of community and ministry in these terms, the church today appears irrelevant to its own Western members, and totally alien to non-Westerners. The bishops present at those synods in Rome, from all the countries around the world, but especially from the southern hemisphere, have echoed the same refrain: "The church is alien to our countries" (Pimenta 1983).

If this represents a megatrend in the church, then the answer in mission, according to Avery Dulles, must be the *development of a global church* (Dulles 1988b, 34-50). The movement toward such a church seems already to have begun. Numerically, the majority of the Catholics are already in non-Western countries. By the year 2000, Walbert Bühlmann has estimated, seventy percent of Catholics will be in third-world countries.

Qualitatively, many of the new trends in the church have originated in, or have been inspired by, the "mission churches": the quest for liturgical renewal, for ecumenism and interfaith dialogue, the movement for inculturation and being true to one's own identity, the new understanding of ministry and the establishment of new ministries are a few of them. Many of the developments that have taken place in the Catholic Church are the fruit of the churches in third-world countries (Metz 1981).

This global church envisioned for the future must be universal and at home in any local culture. It must be incarnated at the local level, and also in dialogue with the world. And Rome becomes the focal point for dialogue and service. It is the focal point of dialogue, because it calls all the incarnated churches in the world to sharing together, to enriching one another, to challenging one another. It is the focal point for service, because it coordinates and motivates the efforts of the local churches and their experiments to make Christianity meaningful to each culture and people. In order to develop that global church, we need bridge-builders, people who have lived in both types of churches, in different cultures, so that there can be a flow of knowledge, of experience and of innovation among the churches.

Globalization

The sixth megatrend consists of all the incipient efforts being made by many human beings and by groups, towards a socio-economic political globalism. The world has become a small village. Today all peoples are living together: they are interdependent and must either learn how to live together in daily life, how to deal peacefully and creatively with one another's culture, customs, traditions, ways of life, or they may die together. There is no longer the possibility of political domination of one people over another. Though the possibility of economic and military domination is still an option, it is becoming less and less available. The examples of Russia in Afghanistan and in Eastern Europe, and of the U.S.A. in Vietnam and in Central America, clearly demonstrate that the day of political domination by one people over another is coming to an end. In this global village which the world has become, human beings must live and learn how to work together, to share with one another, and to appreciate one another, or they may bring this civilization to a tragic end. Rev. Thomas Clarke remarked in *America* that even if the atomic bomb may never be used for political, economic, and military reasons, it may be used on account of cultural misunderstandings.

If there is a megatrend towards globalism, the response in mission must be *universalism.* Universalism means the acceptance of all peoples, respect and veneration for all cultures, welcoming the input from all persons and groups of good will, readiness to receive and to learn, eagerness to share, willingness to be corrected and to be complemented. Universalism not only means opening our windows to the outside, but keeping them wide open, so that the mutuality between our church and other churches, religions, all sorts of movements for the good of God's kingdom, is not stopped, but continues with unrelenting determination.

The Poor as the New Evangelizers

The seventh megatrend is constituted by the centrality of the poor and oppressed in the plan of God for humanity — God's poor — namely, those who own nothing and have no power, but possess a great faith and greater love — as they struggle to change their situation. These poor are once again at the center of our understanding of God's plan for humanity. Once more, God has chosen them to evangelize the world, to help the world to come to a new understanding of the gospel, of the real values of life, of the true value of community, of the joy of sharing. This is evident in Latin and Central America, in the Philippines, and in all the countries where the majority of the population is poor and oppressed, and yet, in the power of their faith and their commitment to love, they struggle to change that situation, and to bring about a better world for all. God has chosen these people to reveal the gospel anew to humanity, to once more announce the good news to the human family of God.

If this is a megatrend, the response in mission must be a *preferential option for the poor*. Missionaries sent to areas where the poor are the majority, and a good percentage has become conscientized, must be able to live with them, understand and appreciate their values, learn from their examples, and follow their style of evangelization. And since most of those who make this option, who identify with the poor, who live and minister with them, are cross-cultural ministers, the example they set to the church of learning from the poor, sharing with them, joining them in their struggle, has a very special meaning for all.

New Presence and Significance of Women

An eighth megatrend with a decisive influence on society is the new awareness of the presence of women in the life of the church and society. This influences biblical studies which read and interpret God's word through the eyes of women. Done thus, theology acquires new, much more clearly nuanced perceptions. Spirituality is lived and expressed in different modes or finds a uniquely womanly expression. Ministry sees its deepest revolution ever, and pastoral theology calls the church to an entirely new level of self-awareness and praxis. Psychology is reviewed with special insights, and within very different experiences. The liturgy is prepared and acted out with touches of beauty and refinement rarely experienced before, and the whole church's atmosphere is pregnant with newness and creativity. The irruption of women as partners in the life and activities of the church and its mission is starting a new era, a better era, an exciting era.

My own more recent experience in ministry in Nairobi and Kenya readily confirms what I have expressed above. Amani Counseling Center, where I do part-time counseling, is run almost entirely by women who are extremely competent and totally dedicated. CHIEA, where I teach, has experienced new life and healthy competition, with the admission of women, who are among the best students and the most active members of the university community. At St. Michael's in Otiende, where I celebrate Mass on Sunday, the women direct the singing, are the backbone in the teaching of cate- chism, and the soul of the parish council. Wherever I go in Kenya for talks or retreats, women are found in all types of situations, and are considered true ministers of the church and its mission.

The response in mission to this megatrend can only be *equality, partner- ship, co-responsibility, and co-ministry.* An answer from the church less than full acceptance and full partnership would not be acceptable by a society where women more and more are seen as equal partners. The church today is keenly aware of St. Paul's strong words: "There are no more distinctions between Jew and Greek, slave and free, male and female, but all are one in Christ Jesus" (Gal. 3:28).

New Frontiers for Mission

Finally, the ninth megatrend with a direct bearing upon mission: the rapid increase in the number of people who have not been exposed to the Christ event. Population studies done by Dr. David Barrett indicate that the number of Christians may decrease within the next fifty years from one- third of the world population in 1970, to one-fourth in the year 2000, and one-fifth in the year 2020 (Bühlmann 1990, 6-7). Conversely, the number of those who have not been exposed to, or have not had an adequate opportunity to learn of, the Christ event is increasing rapidly, "indeed, since the end of the Council it has almost doubled" (R.M. 3, 31, 40). For Chris- tians who understand what God has done for the whole world in and through Jesus Christ, this is a shattering piece of information.

The response in mission must be *missio ad extra,* mission outside and beyond the parameters of the church. There must be personnel in the church who are interested in, and concerned with, the new frontiers of the church. That interest and concern are not founded on false theological premises such as "there is no salvation for those outside the church," or "they do not know God," because the experience of every cross-cultural minister contradicts such premises. But the concern and zeal of the mis- sionary must be based on the truth that we are called to share the Christ event with all those who are willing to listen. The need for evangelization is not based on whether or not the explicit knowledge of Jesus saves people, but on what those who know him do with that knowledge (Gorski 1988). The imperative for evangelization is based on the need for sharing on the part of those who are disciples. Otto Maduro, a sociologist of religion from Venezuela, who has served in an advisory capacity with many missionary groups, states:

> Missionary humility, or humility as mission, demands a recognition on the part of the missioner that he or she is sent "not because they are

needed there." No, in the first place, the missioner goes because of love, because in order to become a complete person, he or she needs the other person, culture, and community where they are sent (Maduro 1987, 67).

Co-partnership with the Earth

The earth has lately emerged into the consciousness of millions of people as the first sacrament of God's love for its inhabitants, as the womb which gives life and nurtures it constantly, as the partner in the journey of humanity towards the kingdom. The earth can no longer be considered as an object to be exploited, as something outside the human family, as a slave to be controlled and dominated, and as a means to be used and misused as one pleases. The earth is part of humanity, and humans are part of the earth. They have a common destiny. To abuse the earth is to commit suicide, to misuse the earth is to threaten life, to respect the earth and to treasure it as one of God's greatest gifts is to assure life.

The response of the church in mission is to *propose a renewed theology of the earth,* and to *promote ecology in all its aspects,* including the banning of all atomic weapons. If mission has anything to do with life, with quality of life, with the promotion of God's kingdom on earth, and if life and kingdom are not possible unless the earth is venerated as a gift, and considered full partner in the journey of humanity towards that kingdom, then intrinsic to mission there should be a strong ecological component. Bühlmann states that "the ecological question is rapidly becoming problem number one of our century" (Bühlmann 1990, 127). If this is so, then it must become an essential part of mission as soon as possible.

THE ROLE OF CROSS-CULTURAL MINISTERS

If these are the megatrends present in the world and in the church, which affect mission directly and call for something new and different in mission, what future roles are there for missionaries in cross-cultural ministry?

To Be Persons of God

If there is a revival of religion in the world, if people are hungry for God, if they strive to establish a deep relationship with God through a holistic spirituality, then a cross-cultural minister must be able to help them in that journey. But no effective help can be given unless they themselves are imbued with this spirituality, and have made a personal encounter with God which has given them a totally new orientation in life, and a radically new view of everything that exists in the light of that encounter. Missionaries must refocus this essential part of their mission, and give it an absolute priority, so that the God whom people are seeking may be found by them, and be the God of Jesus and of the poor.

To Be Global

The second role of a missionary is to be a global person, and thus become a forerunner of what all human beings on earth are called to become, as we move closer to a global existence. Missionaries must be persons who live in, or have lived in, more than one culture, who have made contact with more than one nation, who have prayed with disciples of more than one religion. They have learned more than one language. They are at home everywhere, but not quite at home anywhere. They are persons who can move easily from one place to another, from one culture to another, and not become confused, or lost, or incapable of action.

As humanity moves closer to a world community, only those individuals who have developed these qualities and skills that the missionary ought to possess and become an example of, will be able to live in that global village, grow, operate, and be happy. People who cannot accept multiculturalism, multiracism, people who are afraid of moving from one place to another, from one culture to another, people who cannot master more than one language will find it hard to live the next stage of human existence. Today's missionary is the type of what all people must become in the next era of the development of humanity.

To Be Bridge-Builders

The third role of today's missionary is that of a bridge-builder between cultures, religions, and peoples. I have said earlier that the resurgence of culturalism, and the revival of religions are megatrends. I added that the church must respond to them through inculturation and interfaith dialogue. Missionaries are the obvious ones to foster dialogue between cultures, religions, churches, and peoples, because they have experienced and have lived in more than one culture, have become acquainted with more than one religious tradition, have been exposed to more than one way of life, have experienced more than one set of values. Such persons can become bridges that unite cultures, religions, and values; they can interpret for their own people these different values, these strange customs, these exotic cultures, and these unacceptable religions. Missionaries are the ideal ones to bridge humanity as it moves towards the new era of its history.

Catalysts between Local Churches

The fourth role of missionaries is to become catalysts between local Catholic churches. The global church we envision is formed by the communion of all the local churches in the various continents, in the varied cultures of the world. Each of these churches is at home in the culture of its people, incarnates the whole life of the Lord and his gospel, lives it and manifests it in nuances which are different, because each is rooted in a different culture. Hence, local churches must come into contact with, dialogue with, challenge each another. The churches which are experimenting with new ways of community, of religious life, or ministry must come to a point where they can share with others the riches of their discoveries, and where new experiments can be placed under the scrutiny not of any single incarnated church, but of all churches gathered together, whose decisions will be inspired by the gospel and the living traditions of the believing community. There must be people in the church who have gained experience in different churches, who can mediate these new ways into the life of other Christian communities, helping to incorporate the values discovered in the churches they have served, even challenging the sending church by reporting on forms of worship, of religious life, of community, experienced elsewhere, which have proven life-giving for the community of believers. There must be people who are catalysts among the inculturated churches, and missionaries are these people.

Promoters of New Ministries

The fifth role of missionaries is to be the forerunners of new and different ministries, and above all of a different style of ministry. In the Western church, ministry finds itself in deep crisis, to which, for the time being, there is no solution. To insist on proposing only, or mainly, the type of ministry traditional to the Western church is to go counter to the movement of the Spirit, to close our eyes to the evidence of the facts, to betray the expectations of the people, and to make void the many new opportunities available to people in ministry. Missionaries to the churches of the southern hemisphere, working with the small faith communities, have experienced the richness of new ministries. They have witnessed the effectiveness of these new ministries. The people of God, for their part, have seen their young churches grow and develop, mainly through the services of dedicated lay ministers.

Above all, some missionaries themselves have developed a totally different style of ministry, a ministry based on service and dialogue, on the empowerment of people, on the recognition of the gifts granted by the Spirit to the members of the community. Having experienced these new ministries, and a different style of ministry, they can render a great service to the Western church by promoting awareness of these new forms of service to God's people elsewhere, and by awakening their own local church to the value of this new style of ministry.

Friends of the Poor

The sixth role consists in the fact that missionaries are friends of the poor and the oppressed. Over the centuries, missionaries have been many things to millions of people around the world. They have been teachers, ministers, promoters of development, benefactors; they have been organizers; but seldom have they been friends. I remember a talk given by an SVD missionary at a mission congress in Baltimore. His main thesis was that missionaries have been everything to millions of people, except their friends. If that was true in the past, it can no longer be true in mission in the future. Unless missionaries are true friends to their own people as well as all others, there is little room for them in the world. But this friendship is due primarily to the poor and the oppressed. The missionary of the future must be a friend of the poor, must learn from them, experience their situation, their humiliations, their powerlessness, as well as the riches of their faith, and the tremendous values of their communities. This friendship will help both the missionary and the poor because "few methods are more liberating than asking the oppressed about their experience, memory, and vision of their own history" (Maduro 1987, 67).

It is from the poor that missionaries must relearn the gospel, genuine human values, including "the ability to enjoy life in all its simplicity" (70). As friends of the poor, they must become their partners in the struggle for a better world, for greater justice and equality in this world. This struggle must be carried out in both camps, not only in the mission country, working side by side with the poor, but also in the countries from which they come.

If this is a duty for all missionaries, it is an even greater responsibility for missionaries from the countries of the northern hemisphere. These countries, with their enormous wealth, military power, and political influence, are one of the major causes of the poverty in the world, and often become the supporters of oppressive regimes. Reverse mission as promotion of justice through changing unjust structures in the rich countries is a necessary component of mission. Maduro expresses it well when he states:

> We must enable them [returned missionaries] to connect with currents and movements which seek to reshape the role of the northern countries in a liberating direction toward the Third World . . . If mission is merely reduced to "doing good for the poor," leaving the structures of power unquestioned and intact, then mission will be anything but a liberating project for the oppressed of this world (74-75).

Several mission institutes have adopted the policy of reverse mission, and many missionaries have been called back home to carry out this type of mission.

Partners with Women

Missionaries who have chosen to become members of churches in the Third World, and who are aware of the dignity and vocation of women, of their hard work in those churches, and also of the treatment they receive from society and the church itself, must assume totally different attitudes in their relationship towards women, and develop a very different style of ministry in their regard. Pope John Paul II highlights the dignity and vocation of women, as well as the gratitude of the church towards them, for all they are and mean to it:

The dignity and the vocation of women—a subject of constant human and Christian reflection—have gained exceptional prominence in recent years. This can be seen, for example, in the statement of the Church's Magisterium present in various documents of the Second Vatican Council, which declares in its Closing Message: "The hour is coming, in fact has come, when the vocation of women is being acknowledged in its fullness, the hour in which women acquire in the world an influence, an effect and a power never hitherto achieved. That is why, at this moment when the human race is undergoing so deep a transformation, women imbued with the spirit of the Gospel, can do so much to aid humanity in not falling" (*Mulieris Dignitatem* 1).

Missionaries, according to the pope, must acquire the same attitudes as Jesus in their relationships with women:

This meaning [of the dignity and vocation of women] becomes clearer for us from Christ's words, and from his attitude towards women, an attitude which is extremely simple, and for this very reason extraordinary, if seen against the background of his time. It is an attitude marked by great clarity and depth. Various women appear along the path of the mission of Jesus of Nazareth, and his meeting with each of them is a confirmation of the evangelical "newness of life" already spoken of. It is universally admitted—even by people with a critical attitude towards the Christian message—that in the eyes of his contemporaries Christ became a promoter of women's true dignity and of the vocation corresponding to this dignity (12).

Missionaries must also be aware that, in most of the countries where they work, the situation of women is far from just, and radical redress is called for. Through their attitudes, their efforts to integrate women in all spheres of the church's life and activities on a basis of equality and full partnership, missionaries ought to accelerate the time when the women of the Third World will claim for themselves the dignity and the rights which God has granted all humans.

Searchers of New Frontiers

Another role of missionaries, as they try to respond to the megatrends which affect the church's mission, is to explore new frontiers. Actually, this is the specific role of personnel in cross-cultural situations. Missionaries are disciples with a keen interest in the unreached. They are ministers on the unexplored frontiers of the church. To be faithful to its vocation as sent, the church must always go beyond the boundaries secured, push them back sharing the good news of God with all peoples, and promoting the kingdom of God in the spirit of that good news.

It is not the church which promotes the growth of the church. It is not the disciples who make disciples. That is the work of the Holy Spirit. Members of the church are called to proclaim the good news, and, through their services, to contribute to the progress of the kingdom. The Spirit decides whose mind to open, and on whom to bestow the gift of faith. Yet the Spirit cannot choose new disciples unless these have already encountered the good news brought by the old disciples. The Spirit cannot expand the church, unless the disciples break through existing boundaries towards new frontiers, beyond the established church.

It is up to us to proclaim; it is up to the Spirit to choose who will accept our proclamation. It is up to us to go out; it is up to the Spirit to bring the going to fulfillment. It is up to us to broadcast the Word; it is up to the Spirit to kindle the faith that accepts the Word.

Community-Minded People

The Spirit of God has inspired the establishment of small faith communities as the normal way of belonging to the church, and the most effective way of promoting togetherness, belongingness, mutual help and support in the struggle for a better world. This phenomenon began in the churches of the southern hemisphere, and it is still going very strong. All the synods have praised this movement of the Spirit, all the churches which have experienced it have nothing but praise for it, and all the peoples who have belonged to one of such communities are ready to testify that in and through them they have renewed their faith in God and their commitment to justice.

From the very beginning, missionaries have been part of this movement, and most of them have also promoted it with conviction and determination. All missionaries, and especially the future missionaries, cannot but follow this trend, and dedicate themselves to forming small faith communities which are alive in the Spirit, and active in the world. To do this, they must be community-minded, feel part of each community they belong to, participate in the life and activities of these communities, be ready to share with their members, to walk with them in humility and in mutuality, and be willing to learn from all members who are inspired by the Spirit.

Earthly People

Missionaries have been living with people who have a deep sense of veneration for the earth, a great respect for the earth, and all its creatures, who have made of the earth not only a partner in their journey, but also a means of celebration. Whether they lived with native Americans, or aborigines, tribal people, members of ancient and developed cultures and religions, they always have experienced this love for the earth, and this full participation of the earth in the life and celebrations of them all. There is no dualism among them. There is no sense of superiority between them and the earth.

At present these same missionaries are experiencing the decline of the veneration of the earth, of respect for its creatures by the natives themselves, but more so by big business. The desire for wealth, the thirst for money enkindled in the natives by the gigantic corporations, the need to provide cash for the family and its necessities, have trained natives to squander the most beautiful lands, and have contributed to the killing of most animals. It has created havoc where there was harmony, and devastation where there existed order.

These missionaries who, in the past, had witnessed the beauty of the earth in many lands, and how this earth is treasured and venerated by their people, can become the forerunners of the ecological movement, and make it part and parcel of mission. If the mission of the church does not include this component, and if the ecological movement does not have a deep religious motivation, the earth will continue to be threatened, its life will become more and more difficult for all, and its religious nature will be blurred to the point of no return.

CONCLUSION

The church lives in the world and is part of the world, while at the same time it transcends it with its perennial gospel values. The rootedness in the gospel gives the church a common basis on which all believers concur, and its perennial existence in and through history. The rootedness in the world gives the church its historicity and its provisional existence at any given time in history. It is this rootedness in the world which makes the context important to the church and its mission. While the gospel offers the spirit with which the church lives and operates, the context offers the historical nuances of its life and operations. Both are important, and both should be kept in mind when sharing the church and its mission.

The megatrends I have briefly described provide this contextualization for the reflections which I will offer in the following chapters. They will give directions to those in mission; and they, in turn, will have to discern with the community whether the directions are in keeping with the essentials of the gospel or not. The context is a point of departure, and it is essential because it offers the experience of people who journey under the inspiration of the Spirit. The communal reflection of the believers, in the light of the scripture and of the social sciences, is equally important, because it confirms directions for believers.

2

THE EMERGING GLOBAL CHURCH

The church is a divine reality and a human institution; it is mystery and history. This is probably one of the reasons for the great interest aroused by the church in our world. All its facets are subject to study by historians, sociologists, anthropologists, psychologists, writers, poets and, of course, theologians. The result of this intense interest in the church is evidenced by the research conducted, the studies done, the volumes upon volumes published.

The perspective of this chapter is theological-pastoral, within a global context. Probably this combined approach may produce something new, or at least something that will generate new enthusiasm in pastoral agents who serve the world as the church's representatives.

I intend to present a renewed, if not new, vision of the church, which is in keeping with the world realities, and the church's own universality regained at Vatican II, and subsequent synods of the bishops. I will do this by reviewing very briefly the teachings of Vatican II and post-Vatican II documents of the magisterium, and some of the latest Catholic theological publications on the subject. After that, I will attempt to sketch a description of the most prevalent vision and model of the church as it is all over the world, despite some different models which exist side by side with it. A question will then be raised: Is this overall vision of the church still valid, given its own and the world's new realities? To those who give a negative answer to this question, I will offer a short description of another emerging vision of the church, which could substitute for the prevalent one if this seems obsolete and no longer in keeping with the world's realities. Finally I will reflect on the impact that such a vision could have on the churches of the Third World, as they strive to become true local churches.

VATICAN II AND POST-VATICAN II OFFICIAL TEACHING

The fathers of the council proposed several understandings of the church, and several essential elements for its internal life and for its mis-

17

sion. They accepted a pluriformity of theological interpretations of this mystery, which can never be fully understood and, even less, adequately described. They felt comfortable with this pluralism, and used the several concepts of church as they seemed best to fit the realities of the world, or as they served best the church's members and its mission in the world.

Primarily a Mystery

In its origin, in its internal life, in its holiness, in its deepest reality the church is a mystery, beyond human reach. It is the daughter of the Father, the bride of Christ, the spouse of the Spirit, the temple of God. It is endowed with all sorts of charisms given by the Spirit, it is the new Jerusalem, the house of God in which God's family resides, the mystical body of Christ (L.G. 1-9; R.M. 9).

People of God

This is probably the most comprehensive understanding of church in Vatican II. All peoples are loved by God. In various ways all are brought into communion with God in and through Jesus, all are saved by God, all are God's family (L.G. 9-17; R.M. 4, 5, 10).

Community and Communion of Local Churches

The church is the sacrament of union with God (D.V. 61-64). The church is *koinonia,* and gathers peoples of all races, nations, and tribes to help them live in unity. The church is and makes communion (L.G. 1): is communion of all gifts, of all peoples, of all services, of all vocations, of all local communities which incorporate the fullness of its being, and yet need to be linked with one another, and with the sign and center of communion, the pope, to be fully church (L.G. 14-16; G.S. 22; E.N. 61-62).

Sacrament and Proclaimer of the Kingdom

It is a sign of all that God wants for humanity and for the world, all that God has done for them, all that God expects of them. And, at the same time, the church announces, keeps alive all the hopes and concerns of God's kingdom. The kingdom is the absolute; the church is its sign and its herald (G.S. 1-3; E.N. 8). The kingdom is where God operates salvation, and the church must be present and operative in it (G.S. 40-45), so that this salvation may have all the qualities of life present in the Trinity, and its development may be holistic—that is, personal (G.S. 12-22; E.N. 35), communitarian (G.S. 23-32; E.N. 29), and global (G.S. 33-39; E.N.18).

In this context the church is also seen as *diakonia,* as service to the world in all its needs, beauty, sinfulness. The church has to be at the disposal of all needs of the human family of God (R.H. 1314; E.N. 31; R.M. 19), to be an agent of ecumenism (U.R. 4; E.N. 77; R.M. 50), to be a promoter of religious freedom (D.H. 2; E.N. 39, 53; R.M. 39), to champion the cause of the poor (G.S. 67, 69; R.M. 37b), to support the cultures of the world (G.S. 53-62; E.N. 20, 63), to actively foster peace and a new world order (G.S. 63-90; R.M. 37c).

Institution

The church is also an institution, a historical entity, living amid the world. At times the church is affected by the spirit of the world and the way this operates. It is fully aware of its human and institutional deficiencies, of its limitations, of its sinfulness, of the need to be liberated and redeemed by God, as any other institution, of the necessity for *metanoia* and for evangelization *ad intra* (L.G. 8, 15; G.S. 43; E.N. 15).

Local Church

Vatican II ushered in the official recognition of local churches (C.D. 11; L.G. 23, 26; A.G. 22; E.N. 62). In these local or particular churches, the church of Christ exists, it is fully present:

In these communities, though frequently small and poor, or living far from one another, Christ is present. By virtue of Him, the one, holy, catholic and apostolic Church gathers together (L.G. 26).

These local churches must be rooted in the life and culture of the people, so as to mirror the latter in their own lives, and to reveal them in their own activities. The local people ought to be able to recognize themselves in their church, and to recognize their church in themselves (A.G. 19, 22; L.G. 13). These local churches must be, as much as possible, self-reliant in all aspects of their life and mission, and yet each of them should support the others and be helped by them, always in union with the center and sign of unity among all of them, the vicar of Christ (A.G. 19, 22; E.N. 64; R.M. 85). Neither separation, nor uniformity, but communion in plurality is the vision of Vatican II for the existence of the local churches, and their relationship to the universal church and its center.

Signs of the Times Revelatory of God's Word

The Word of God is central to the church. The church is gathered by the Word of God proclaimed, is constituted by it, directed by it. The church is gathered by the Word, its life is based on the Word, its mission consists in proclaiming it in all its multiple aspects (D.V. 1, 5, 7, 17; E.N. 13, 14,

15; L.G. 1, 2, 5, 12, 17, 19, 20; P.O. 2, 4; S.C. 6, 9, 24, 33, 35; A.G. 3-7, 13-15).

The Word of God is not a static reality in the life of the church, but dynamic. Its full meaning is better understood through the events of history, through the experiences of people:

> The Tradition that comes from the Apostles makes progress in the Church with the help of the Holy Spirit. There is a growth in insight into the realities and words that are being passed on . . . By means of the same Tradition . . . the Holy Scriptures themselves are more thoroughly understood and actualized in the Church (D.V. 8).

The truth of the Word of God is not abstract, but rooted in words and actions, related to the events of history; all of which finds its apex in the revelation of the Word of God himself, in the person of Jesus (D.V. 4). History becomes the locus of God's ongoing revelation, and is itself revelatory of God. With this renewed insight the church, as envisioned by the fathers of Vatican II, is not only focused on sacraments and ministries, but also on the living Word of God in the scriptures and in tradition, explicated by God's signs of the time. These signs guide the church in its renewal, in its own understanding, in its mission (G.S. 4).

Renewed Church Structures in the Light of God's Signs

The church as a divinely instituted entity does not change. God who instituted it will keep it in being as God wishes it. The church holds its being also from Christ and the Spirit, and their presence in the church keeps it undefiled and holy. But the church as a historical institution has to respond to the signs of the time, and modify its contingent existence, structures, and mission accordingly, in order to be existentially what it is ontologically. The changing of its own understanding, of its visible existence and structures, is a requirement of its faithfulness to Christ and the Spirit who continually call it to be in history what it is in essence: a luminous sign of their presence in the world.

One of the major structural changes called for by Vatican II was collegiality in the church among bishops and the pope (L.G. 22-24), and between clergy and laity (L.G. 37). This collegiality does not infringe upon the authority proper to the various leaders of the church, but offers a more Christlike approach to its use and its sharing.

In conclusion we can say that Vatican II called the church to renewal: a renewal faithful to the church's divine essence, but also open and commensurate to the new situations of the world. This renewal was to be accomplished in a pluriform and not a univocal way, following the pluriformity of understandings and approaches to the church and its mission. The relationship among the members of the church, and between them and the rest of the world, and the structures of the church, would be most affected by this call to renewal. Radical changes were proposed to accomplish this relational and structural renewal.

Moved by this impetus and animated by this motivation, the whole church plunged into a feverish movement of renewal. And the theologians accompanied these efforts towards renewal with further reflections on the church, advancing the teachings of the council, and sometimes even straying from its teachings.

THEOLOGICAL REFLECTIONS

To summarize even the major theological writings would be impossible in one chapter of one book, and above all it would be outside the scope of this book. I shall therefore sketch very briefly those elements of the literature which will help the purpose of the chapter: to give a panoramic view of the reflections on the church of theologians from the various continents, in order to prepare the grounds for a description and an understanding of the emerging church.

Avery Dulles

In his classic book *Models of the Church,* Dulles identifies five models of church.

The first model stresses primarily the external, juridical aspects of the church (Dulles 1974, 31-42). The church is a perfect society, with all the constitutive elements of a society bestowed by Christ. The beneficiaries of this model are the juridical members of the institution (38). The mission of this type of church is "to save their [nonmembers] souls precisely by bringing them into the institution" (38).

The church in the mystical communion model (43-57) is considered primarily as "an informal and interpersonal community" (43), characterized by a horizontal dimension, the divine life disclosed by the incarnate Christ and communicated to all through his Spirit (44-45). The beneficiaries are the members but understood not in a juridical sense, but in a more spiritual sense, as those animated by supernatural faith and charity (53). The goal of the church as Mystical Body is to "lead men into communion with the divine" (54).

The institutional and the spiritual elements of the church, which, stressed independently, may lead to risky conclusions, are harmonized in the sacramental model of the church (58-70). The church as a sacrament must signify in a historically tangible form the redeeming grace of Christ (63). As sacrament the church has an outer and an inner aspect or reality: the outer is the institution, which makes the church visible; the inner is the spiritual element, which makes it divine (63-64). The beneficiaries of the church are "all those who are better able to articulate and live their faith, thanks to their contact with the believing and loving Church" (67). The goal or mission of the church then is to "purify and intensify men's response to the grace of Christ" (67).

This ecclesiology of the herald model sees the church as gathered and formed by the Word of God. It is a kerygmatic community heralding to the whole world all God's deeds, especially those done in Jesus Christ (71-82). The beneficiaries of this model are "all those who hear the Word of God and put their faith in Jesus as Lord and Savior" (78). The goal or mission of the church is to herald the message, to "proclaim all that the Church has heard, believed and been commissioned to proclaim" (71).

The servant model of the church is seen as part of the world, accepting the world's own proper autonomy, learning from the world and, above all, serving it (83-96). This model ushers in a secular-dialogical theology:

Secular, because the Church takes the world as a properly theological locus, and seeks to discern the signs of the times; dialogical, because it seeks to operate on the frontier between the contemporary world and the Christian tradition (including the Bible), rather than simply apply the latter as a measure of the former (86).

Beneficiaries are "all those brothers and sisters the world over, who hear from the Church a word of comfort or encouragement, or who obtain from the Church a respectful hearing, or who receive from it some material help in their hour of need" (91). The goal or mission of the church is to be of help to all, to keep alive the hope and aspirations of all for God's kingdom and its values, and in the process to be offering guidance and criticism.

In *The Reshaping of Catholicism*, Dulles refers to what we could consider another model of church: the emergent world church (Dulles 1988b, 36-50). Drawing from Karl Rahner and Walbert Bühlmann, Dulles offers just a glimpse of this emerging church. Then he goes on developing the theory of inculturation. It is a pity that he has not dwelt more on the subject of world church. It is this type of church that I will propose later.

Walbert Bühlmann

Bühlmann has written several books on the church. The most important ones are *The Coming of the Third Church* and *The Church of the Future*.

In *The Coming of the Third Church*, Bühlmann maintains that there are three churches living side by side. The first church is the oriental church, and the church of silence in communist countries. They are fixed in the past, and with very little influence on the present (Bühlmann 1977, 8-12). The second church is the Western church. It experiences a decline in membership and in ministers, and it is undergoing a deep crisis as is the whole Western world (13-18). The third church is the one in the southern hem-

isphere where Catholics are already the majority of the church's membership and growing fast, where ministers are increasing, and whose
importance seems to match that of the whole hemisphere for the future of
the world (19-24). After a short description of these three churches, Bühlmann looks at several aspects of the life, theology, institutions, and mission
of the church, and proposes changes to meet the challenges of the present
and of the future.

In *The Church of the Future* Bühlmann speaks of a world church, which
is being shaped in the South (Bühlmann 1986, 3-11). He looks with pride
on the emergence of this world church as it exists embryonically in Latin
America (12-27), in Africa (28-42), and in Asia (43-56). He projects that
the churches of the Third World will help the Western church. Then he
proposes different structures which would serve best the world church, and
a renewed sense of mission and unity in the church at large. Finally Karl
Rahner, in the epilogue of this book, proposes new perspectives on pastoral
ministry in the future. In it Rahner speaks of an incipient world church
(190), a globalization in theology and evangelization, and mentions several
pastoral areas which would be affected by a global Christianity (190-97).

Richard P. McBrien

Richard McBrien also talks of models of the church. For him there exist
three models: the church as institution, the church as community, the
church as servant (McBrien 1984, 710-14). Substantially his models are the
same as Dulles's. By contrast, Rahner and Schillebeeckx are strong supporters of sacramental ecclesiology, though each proposes variations to the
model mentioned by Dulles (Dulles 1974, 69). Lately there seems to be a
convergence among them, and among most Western theologians, on the
need to look seriously at the kingdom realities, and take heed of them
(McBrien 1970, 67-85). McBrien summarizes this tendency when he asks:

> Do we then need the Church? The answer is "Yes" only if we view
> the Church for the sake of the reign of God ... The world, in the
> final accounting, needs a Church which, as an eschatological com-
> munity, never rests until the principles of the Gospel of Jesus Christ
> are everywhere realized and extended (McBrien 1970, 85).

What about the church's structures? "The Church really has no other ethical option than to pursue the path of thoroughgoing institutional reform"
(McBrien 1973, 145).

Leonardo Boff

Boff has written two books on the church: *Church: Charism and Power*,
and *Ecclesiogenesis: The Base Communities Reinvent the Church*. These two

books complement each other, and offer a distinctive vision for a renewed church. Boff first of all presents some models of the church from the past (Boff 1985, 2-7), then he develops his own model which has unique features and vision. Boff believes that "the future is linked to those bishops who allow history to assert its rightful place in the Church" (3). Boff writes to critique the till-now dominant institutional *mater et magistra* vision, which he believes has aligned itself with the powers in control of history to the detriment of the interests of the poor. It believes itself to be working for the poor and educating the masses, but in fact, according to Boff, the effect of its manner of functioning is "to provide for the Church's [own institutional] needs and guarantee its existence" (4).

A model called *the sacrament of salvation* model by Boff stresses the problem of development. For Boff, a church understood in this manner entered the world to take part in development: "The principal problems were not doctrinal or liturgical [but] linked to society: justice, social participation and internal development for everyone" (5-6). In this struggle for development, according to Boff, the church "denounced the abuses of the capitalist system and the marginalization of the poor. However, it did not present an alternative perspective, but a reformist one [that was] acceptable to the dominant sectors of society" (6). The future of the sacrament of salvation model and of its mission in the world, a mission which Boff sees as being carried out in close cooperation with the "modern" sectors of society, is dependent on the future of *that* society (7).

By way of contrast with the foregoing two models, Boff presents as his own proposal a new model: *the church of the poor.* It is a strikingly revolutionary view in which the church is envisioned "from the bottom up," as imaged primarily at the grass roots among the marginalized. The church of the poor is in sharp contrast to a church envisioned "from above" (Boff 1986, chapters 2 and 6). Boff advocates, in fact, tearing down ecclesiastical structures that he views as contrary to the spirit of the Gospel (chapter 4), proposing instead an alternative view of church as the *sacrament of the Holy Spirit:*

> The Church must be thought of not so much as beginning with the Risen Lord, now in the form of the Spirit, but rather as beginning with the Holy Spirit, as the force and means by which the Lord remains present in history, and so continues his work of inaugurating a new world (150).

For this church Boff prescribes "an alternate structure: charism as the organizing principle" (154). Among the charisms there is also that of order and unity (160) but canon law would have a much-diminished role. The new style of church is, then, the community of the oppressed, animated by the Spirit, sustained by charisms, and organized for liberation.

This church is described at length in *Ecclesiogenesis.* Here Boff offers theological reflections, draws graphs, asks difficult questions, and concretizes his vision of the shape of this model of church. Boff adopts a Latin American perspective, but he does so without disregarding the wider the church.

This short review of some of the most salient concepts of church contained in Vatican II, and of models of church presented by several theologians, has shown a pluriform understanding of church, and has also offered elements which will be utilized later, to build a renewed or different vision of church, a vision which will be in keeping with world and church realities, I hope.

3

WESTERN OR GLOBAL CHURCH?

I will speak of the "Western" church in preference to the "institutional" church because that term connotes the exact area where it developed. This church was formed in western Europe. This church, in its present existence, is the daughter of Europe, of European civilization.

This church, born in the West, rooted itself in the Greco-Roman culture, and it became European by absorbing all aspects of that culture. This was good, and natural. We have to accept and admit it. The church which predominates in Catholicism at present exists, operates, and legislates as a European institution, thinks with the categories of European philosophy and theology, celebrates its mysteries with signs and symbols meaningful to European people (at least at one time), and adopted the deductive methodology of theologizing proper to the European mentality. The place of birth, and the assumption of local cultural elements in the church's life, is nobody's fault.

The unstated assumption of this "Western church" carries even deeper implications for our discussion. It implies a spirit, a set of attitudes, a way of relationship, a modus operandi which can be summarized in a short expression: *sense of superiority*. The Western church thinks that its present form of existence is superior to any other form of church; that the way it operates now is probably the best; that its members and leaders who, up to a few years ago, were white and Western, were the best, and cannot be outdone by others; that this church has answers, and the last word, on all subjects, and the rest of the world has little to contribute, but a lot to gain from listening to it and learning from it.

This is the fruit of the birthplace and the original culture of this church. In the West people and leaders always thought that their culture was the superior one, their way of life the best one, their education the most enlightened one, their religion the most divine one. The church absorbed most of these beliefs, attitudes, values, and lived by them. But that process has remained frozen, or undergone very little change, up to this very moment. If anything has to be discussed, it is not *how* the church was formed, or *why* the church exists the way it does. Rather: Why has *this* inculturated model of church become *the* model of church?

MAJOR COMPONENTS OF THE WESTERN CHURCH

The Focus: Its Own Existence

Any institution in the Western world made of itself the center of its attention and activities. Each tried to promote itself, to defend itself, to propagate itself, to assert itself over and above all others. Starting from the Roman Empire, down to the kingdoms and the colonizing powers, this self-centeredness has been most evident. Tacitus describes this forcibly, when he quotes from a Roman governor:

All men have to bow to the command of their betters; it has been decreed by those gods ... that with the Roman people should rest the decision what to give and what to take away, and that they should brook no other judges than themselves (quoted in Wengst 1987, 19).

It seems to me that the focus of the Western church is the church itself. Its major preoccupation is its own life, its own beliefs, its own orthodoxy, its own self, as it exists at present. Karl Rahner says:

In the Church's self-understanding the stress was laid on its "un-changeability." The Church was regarded as the stronghold and sign of what was eternally valid in an increasingly rapidly changing course of history ... On the whole the stress and feeling of self-understanding of the Church were concentrated during this period on unchange-ability (Rahner 1981, 116-17).

Vatican II, especially with its document *Gaudium et Spes,* made gigantic efforts to place the focus of the church more on the world than on itself (G.S. 3, 44, 59, 62, 92). The pope in his travels makes visible this concern, and his talks and encyclicals on social and economic questions stress the importance of the church's involvement in the world. In *Redemptoris Missio* he stresses the importance of the church, but avoids "ecclesiocentrism" (R.M. 19). And yet the Western church seems to retreat more and more into itself, and its activities seem discordant with the original thrust of the council. The rhetoric may still be there, but the reality seems stridently different.

Churches in Other Cultures, a Replica of the Western Church

Western empires, nations, or institutions tried to propagate themselves by making replicas of themselves everywhere they went. They did not change. They remained the same, and imposed their way of life on others, who had to change accordingly. Wengst states that "the Roman way of life spread with the Roman Empire." And he quotes from Tacitus that Agricola in Britain:

> began to train the sons of the chieftains in liberal education ... As a result, the nation which used to reject the Latin language, began to aspire to rhetoric: further, the meaning of our dress became a distinction, and the toga came into fashion, and little by little the Britons were seduced into alluring vices: pillared halls, baths and choice banquets. The simple natives gave name of "culture" to this factor of slavery (Wengst 1987, 41).

The Western church, in its missionary thrust, was transplanted to every other continent. The new churches, though, were replicas of the Western church in every respect. What was done in the West, was repeated everywhere else; what was taught in the West, was echoed elsewhere; the way the community was organized and run in the West, became the pattern everywhere else.

Karl Rahner has expressed criticism of this phenomenon in a particularly clear fashion:

> one can consider the official activity of the Church in a macroscopic way and see clearly that despite the implied contradiction to its essence, the actual concrete activity of the Church in relation to the world outside Europe was in fact (if you will pardon the expression) the activity of an export firm which exported a European religion as a commodity it did not really want to change, but [which was] sent throughout the world together with the rest of the culture and civilization it considered superior (Rahner 1979a, 717).

The necessity of being like the Western church in everything, except perhaps the color of the skin, was drilled with such an intensity and urgency into the minds of its followers that it became a real pride for any church to claim that identity, sameness, uniformity.

The motivation for all this was very lofty. Either the church remained the same or it would no longer be church. Faced with this consequence, even when the local leaders took over the ministry of service in the local churches, it remained a sacred duty to leave things as they were, and not risk betraying the church through changes which would look adulterous (Penoukou 1984, 31-32.). This way of relating by the Western church with its transplanted counterparts in the world made the local people change to fit into its mold, forced the local cultures to modify in the light of the "superior" culture of the West, and many local customs had to be discarded. It was a reverse inculturation! The foreign remained the same: the local had to change into the foreign. The process has left the masses almost untouched, and has brought deep resentment in the educated and the professional class, and is causing a mass exodus from Western-type churches of the Third World.

The Center of the Western Church

The Western institutions were all built and formed around a strong center, which provided for their defense, took care of their members, directed their affairs, and had the last word in all matters. This center was under the direct jurisdiction of one person who, in the Roman Empire was considered as "vicar of God" or "as God on earth" (Wengst 1987, 46-51), and in the European nations was a person with power derived from God. These leaders enjoyed full authority over territories, subjects, and conquered lands. Plutarch says that "Greek cities had as much freedom as the Romans allowed them" (22).

The church also has a center. We Catholics treasure it, and make of it a distinctive mark of our community and of our faith. Historically, though, we have to recognize that its shape and function were influenced tremendously by the Imperial Roman understanding of what an imperial center was supposed to resemble. The church's Roman structure seems to operate in terms of authority, power, and control in much the same way as did the government of the Roman Empire (Césaire, 1972, 9-61).

Dulles notes that "prior to Vatican II it had become quite common to look on the church as a gigantic corporation in which all true authority is located at the top, and flows downwards through the bishops to the laity" (Dulles 1985, 133).

That the church inculturated according to available societal characteristics is not bad; actually "it was necessary for its continuation in the world and, in the theological sense of incarnation, desired by God" (Boff 1985, 40). But to freeze that style in our modern society may create serious difficulties. Dulles observes:

> While society as a whole was becoming democratic and self-critical, the Church became progressively more oligarchic and authoritarian ... connected with this authoritarian development was a second trend: a swing towards absolutism (Dulles 1987, 112).

Methods of Theologizing

In the West, before the scientific revolution, the method of studies was deductive—from principles to conclusions. One progressed from a dogma functioning as an undoubtable certainty to new ideas; one progressed from definitions to practical applications and from there to pronouncements on reality.

Such a theological and ecclesiastical system made conclusions and practices "perennial," "universal," and "unchangeable." And so all over the world, the same theology was taught, the same books were used, the same catechism was memorized.

It is evident that I have made broad generalizations. There have been numerous exceptions in all areas mentioned above. But even these negative features were the fruits of inculturation and had positive sides also. They were historically acceptable, perhaps even meaningful and necessary. As Leonardo Boff states: "Where there is power, there may be abuses of that authority. But we must remember that the majority of those in authority in the Church are men of good faith, clear conscience, impeccable personal character" (Boff 1985, 39). But to continue using the same system when the realities of the world and of the church are totally different may create a serious dilemma. And that is the question I am going to address now.

Is This Vision of the Church Still Valid?

Many writers speak of the end of an era in society—an end of Westernization, an end of the bourgeois age, and an end of the national security state. Some speak of a new era, the global era, a unity of creation era, where boundaries will be blurred and barriers broken down in the church and in the world. This new era can be called an era of *globalization,* or *universalism.* This is the one megatrend in society which will influence all the others. Our world is moving towards this new phase of existence, in which all peoples are neighbors and all will either learn how to live together or die together. The new world order for all aspects of life on this planet is based on this irreversible movement. In this projected new world order, all cultures will have a place, all religions an altar. Freedom will be treasured, the dignity of all respected, interdependence and interaction promoted, pluralism supported, work will be considered a co-creative activity, with a profound spiritual meaning, in union with the earth and the community (Holland 1989, 18-42). This new world order promises to become a new Pentecost which will once again defeat the Babel of division (Osthathios 1980, 35-36). In a world which is called to become a global village, for people who are called to live united as God's family, will a church which is predominantly monocultural be a sign of the realities to come? Will that church be able to lead society in the new era? The answer is a resounding no.

Numerically the church's population has shifted considerably. At the beginning of this century over 70 percent of the Catholics lived in the northern hemisphere, and only a little over 20 percent in the southern hemisphere. At present 452 million Catholics live in the South and 333 million in the North. From 1960 to 1980 the Catholics in Europe and North America increased by 66 million (from 267 to 333 million), while in the other continents they almost doubled (from 251 to 452 million). This trend still continues (Bühlmann 1986, 118-20).

The hierarchy has become more indigenous. While in 1960 there were only three Asian and no African cardinals out of 85 altogether, in 1985 out of 120 cardinals fourteen were Africans, eleven Asians, four from Oceania, and twenty from Latin America. A good increase, but not proportionate to the percentage of Catholics (120-21). In 1951 there were two African bishops and 31 Asians; in 1981 there were 293 African and 408 Asian bishops in charge of dioceses. In 1990 the number of African bishops reached 487 and of Asian bishops went over five hundred.

In all the churches of the South there is a great ferment for inculturation, for recognition of a local church truly "at home" in their culture and land. In all the churches of the South, especially among intellectuals, there is a deep resentment, strongly expressed in words and actions, against the religious colonialism and neocolonialism of the Western church. One has only to read the proceedings of the several meetings of the Ecumenical Association of Third World Theologians (EATWOT) to hear the voice of rebellion and of repudiation of westernization. One has only to read the theological books such as *Christianity Without Fetishes* or novels such as *The African Boy* to become aware of the animosity and indignation of these writers against the policies of the Western church in third-world countries.

Most mainline churches are experiencing an alarming exodus of members, and are witnessing the establishment of innumerable independent churches or sects. This phenomenon is particularly crucial in Africa. The number of these sects or independent churches is escalating to unimaginable proportions. It seems that one major reason for both the exodus and the mushrooming of these churches is the lack of sensitivity for indigenization of the churches from which the sects have separated.

Surrounded by the above mentioned realities, can a Western church be meaningful in the Southern churches? Can it be acceptable for a long time? Can it be a means for further and genuine growth and progress?

Dulles states that such a church would be "a dead body rather than a living Christian community. It would be an unauthentic sign: a sign of something not really present, and therefore not a sacrament" (1974, 64). The present realities of the world and of the church cannot accommodate a Western type of church, not because it is bad in itself, but because it is an anachronism, a strident contradiction to all that exists in the world and in the church.

Is there another type of church which could be proposed, and which could reflect these realities better, and further them with its own example and mission? This type of church, I suggest, *is* being envisioned by third-world Christians, by their theologians and by their missionaries. Moreover, it is emerging more clearly in small pockets all over the world. The Western church is still the strongest in terms of economic and political power. But this emerging church is developing fast, both in its characteristic dimensions and in its practices.

THE EMERGING CHURCH

In the mid-1970s, I was the executive secretary of the U.S. Catholic Mission Council. I traveled all over the world to give talks on the "global church." Many people, when they heard that term, looked at me with some suspicion. One day a courageous man stood up and asked: "Who are you to give a new title to the church"? My answer was: "I have tried to put into a title the type of church I have experienced in the various continents. The title can perhaps be improved, but the experience can not be changed."

Then Karl Rahner in 1979 used an equivalent term, "world church" (Rahner 1979a). The term "world church" became familiar to theologians and pastoral agents. Some of the traits of this church have been sketched (McBrien 1973, 71-136; Boff 1985, 108-24). Some of its strategies have been envisioned (Penoukou 1984, 43-126; Metz 1981, 67-106), some of the structural changes have been advanced (Bühlmann 1986, 117-72). But, to my knowledge, a short yet fairly complete presentation of what is implied by the *world* or *global* church is still lacking. I shall try to gather together and to interpret: (1) the most important characteristics of this emerging church; (2) the major changes called for in the Western church to allow its full emergence; and (3) the spirit behind it.

The Word

I prefer the term "global church" over "world church" for two reasons. First, to avoid the possible negative connotations attached to the term world. For many Christians, world implies all the negative traits derived from the Greek and especially early Christian thought. These and similar connotations could make the title less acceptable, or even rejected, by some Christians. Second, "global" is a term used in many other areas of knowledge.

The Meaning

The meaning is far more important than the terminology. By global church I mean the community of Catholic Christians open to all cultures, to all ways of life, and to the various religious expressions of the same faith and mysteries. A community which welcomes all peoples with their cultures, values, traditions, customs, celebrations, and rites; a community which agrees to be enriched by all peoples, while it strives to enrich them too. The challenge of this church is not based on any prevalent cultural heritage, but on the gospel as it is understood and lived by the *anawim,* the poor of our age. The global church is a community which exists in the world, responds to the sign of God's times, and does not set up a dichotomy between itself and the world, and also does not accept a total identification with it. It is a community on pilgrimage, to discover God's paths for all. Dulles has noted that we are witnessing the birth of a new kind of multi-cultural Catholicism in which the regional churches will interact, criticize and enrich one another. The global church is a community which is at home everywhere, and is a home for all peoples as they exist in their cultural settings, and as they strive to grow under the inspiration of the Spirit.

Focus of the Global Church

The mission of God on earth has the church as one of its agents. The church exists for its mission. Mission constitutes the church, shapes the church, inspires its actions and its life. By mission here we mean all the involvements and activities of the church marked with two characteristics: the others and the ungospelled. These are two essential elements which cannot be waived. The outwardness, the heterocenteredness, the being for others constitute one prong of mission (R.M. 19-20; Sobrino 1989, 32-33, 61). Enda McDonagh strongly emphasizes this point:

A Christian community is compelled by its very nature as a community and particularly as Christian, to expand and go out of itself, or decline and die. As Christian it is possessed by a vision of reality which it feels impelled to share. It is possessed by a truth which can only be distorted by being hoarded. It is possessed by a life that must be transmitted. It is possessed by a love that by definition goes out to others . . . Given the explosive nature of the gospel message, and the impetus of the indwelling Spirit, the Christian community finds its fulfillment in reaching out to others (McDonagh 1969, 12, 15).

The second component, *mission*, complements the first. Whatever is ungospelled, outside or inside the church, is of concern to the church's mission. The church is centered around "ungospelledness," is focused on it, is concerned about it. This aspect of mission, then, is concerned also with the church's own life, institutions, relationships, and systems. The church is thus the object of its own mission. If and when the church's life, institutions, and actions depart from the gospel message and style, mission must intervene to correct and rectify the deviations.

Relationship of the Global Church with Local Churches

This global church is a communion of local churches, and their relationship is of a unique nature. An individual "church" is not just a local franchise of an international organization, but has a unique relationship to the universal church. The church, where it becomes "church" in the full sense of the term, *is* a local church. All these local churches are supposed to be inculturated, and to become the living expression of the local people's faith and Christian life. The global church respects human cultures as God's gift, and promotes inculturation of all that is gospelled in them. The life of the local church has to mirror the life of the people; the theology of the local church has to be formulated on native categories, philosophies, and wisdom; the liturgy of the local church has to incorporate the signs, symbols, and expressions proper to the people; the communities of the local church have to be structured after the native ones; the ways of living out the faith cannot disregard the conditions of life which existed before the coming of the church, unless they are in direct contradiction with the essentials of the gospel.

Pope John Paul II well spelled out the necessity of inculturation of the local churches when he spoke to the bishops of Ghana in 1980, during his first visit to Africa:

> And so with sincerity and confidence and profound openness to the universal Church, the bishops must carry on the task of inculturation of the gospel of each people ... This work is of God: it is an activity of the living Body of Christ: it is a requirement of the Church (See also R.M. 52).

It would be difficult to find stronger words in support of inculturation than the ones spoken by the holy father. And a few days later, to the bishops of Kenya, the pope expanded on the dynamics of inculturation and its fruits, when faithfully undertaken:

> I am close to you in every undertaking to make the gospel incarnate in the lives and cultures of your people. The inculturation which you rightly promote will truly be a reflection of the Incarnation of the Word when a culture, transformed and regenerated by the gospel, brings forth from its own living traditions original expressions of Christian life, celebration and thought ... Thus not only is Christianity relevant to Africa, but Christ, in the members of his Body, is himself African.

The three major areas of the life of the church must be inculturated by each local church: *theology* (expressions of thought), *liturgy* (expressions of celebration), and *morality* (expressions of Christian life). If this is accepted and practiced, then it follows that there will be pluriformity of theologies, of liturgies, and of moral conduct, stemming out of these original expressions which are based on the living traditions of people. If such a process took place, then, as Metz suggests, the Catholic Church would be "changing from a monocentric church, to a culturally polycentric world church" (Fabella and Torres 1985, 89).

Inculturated churches would respond to the needs for cultural self-identity, and give depth to the roots of Christianity in the hearts of the non-Westerners. Missionaries and religious leaders should, then, no longer wonder, as Fr. Drunont in the novel *The Poor Christ of Bomba,* whether:

> These roadside Christians are really any better than the Tala Tribe? does their faith plunge their hearts, like the roots of a forest tree? or does it just spread on their skins, like the roots of those other trees which spread their roots on the flat ground? (Beti 1983, 189)

Inculturated churches would also give these people pride, and they, in turn, would stop wondering:

> whether the Christian religion really suits us, whether it's really made to the measure of the blacks. I used to believe it firmly ... but now, I am not so sure.

Finally, inculturated churches would not force bishops to say at a synod that "their governments often ask whether our Church is for Italians" (Bühlmann 1986, 122), or that their church "no longer be considered alien to the country" (Pimenta 1983, 7), but they will make bishops happy to state that the face of their cultures and of their peoples are imprinted on the church, and that the church is owned by them and makes them and their peoples proud.

Pope Paul VI, who strongly supported the de-westernization of the church and its indigenization, asked a historic question in his address to all the bishops of Africa, a question which still waits for a full answer: "Must the Church be European, Latin, Oriental ... or must she be African?" (Hickey 1982, 199). When this question is answered positively by all churches, then the global church will truly become the communion of all inculturated churches throughout the world, and its center will deal with them in respect and reverence, knowing that they are true gifts of God.

Center of the Global Church

The global church needs a center, and an active one, even more than the Western church did. This special need arises from several factors which are unique to the global church. In fact the church is spread in all six continents; the majority of the members are no longer Western; it is a communion of inculturated churches, each with its own specific identity, theology, liturgy and way of living out the faith. This geographic universality and pluralism of expressions needs a strong center of unity, of dialogues and coordination. A center of *koinonia* and of *diakonia*. Dulles correctly states:

> Now that Christianity is becoming for the first time truly planetary and culturally pluralistic, it is more important than ever to have a central authority that will keep the regional groupings in communion. The centrifugal forces of social cultural diversity must be counterbalanced by the centripetal attraction of a symbolic focus of unity (1985, 142).

The spirit animating this center is expressed in the teachings and examples of Jesus, and of the first apostolic communities. A few quotes suffice to make the point clear. Jesus washed the feet of his disciples, presented himself as a servant, and asked them to do the same for each other, following his examples (Jn. 13:1-20). Jesus quite openly and unequivocally told his disciples that "he had come not to be served, but to serve" (Mk. 10:45). And Matthew, quoting from Isaiah (42:1-4), depicts the ministry of Jesus as that of a servant (Mt. 12:18-21). Jesus strongly warned his disciples against the misuse of authority:

> You know that among the pagans rulers lord it over them, and their great men make their authority felt. This is not to happen among you. No. Anyone who aspires to be great among you, must be your servant, and anyone who wishes to be first among you, must become your slave (Mt. 20:24-27).

Peter must have been deeply impressed by these words, and in his turn he admonishes the elders of the communities to "shepherd the flock of God ... do not lord it over any group that is entrusted to you" (1 Pet. 5:1-4). Such a spirit will inspire the functions and the activities of the center of the global church in relation to all local churches (Molari 1972, 142-49). In fact, the center functions as a point of unity of all local churches, acts to promote dialogue among all these churches, and to foster coordination of all their major activities.

The center of the global church should share responsibility with local churches by practicing honest and sincere collegiality, respecting the role of episcopal conferences, trusting their leaders, upholding their deliberations. McBrien says:

> The church must put into practice at once its own time-honoured principle of subsidiarity that a higher agency or group never do for a lower agency or group what that lower agency or group can do for itself. There must be a decentralization of power which restores to particular churches their ancient freedom to adapt the discipline of

the Christian life and ministry to their distinctive needs and situation (McBrien 1973, 88).

The center should normally not operate independently of the local churches, any more than local churches should operate independently of the center. In either case there would be an abuse of power, which will lead to serious consequences for the church and its mission. Dulles proposes this mutual dependence in clear terms:

In the perspective of Catholicity, it is important that the Pope, as universal teacher, is not an isolated voice. As Joseph Ratzinger has put it, "precisely because of the inner nature of his [pope's] infallibility, he needs the testimony of the ecumene," that is of bishops who are not just papal delegates or shadows of the Pope, but true pastors of other particular churches ... As understood in contemporary theology, the particular churches and their faithful are not merely passive subjects upon whom truth is impressed from outside. As active bearers of the faith, they will often nuance and enrich the very doctrines that they accept on the word of authoritative teachers (Dulles 1985, 144).

Similarly, Josef Ratzinger wrote in the early 1960s:

While the pope is accorded ordinary episcopal power in the whole Church, so that one might not have the impression that the bishops were only executive organs of this power, it is declared on the other hand that they are "instituted by the Holy Ghost" (Denz. 1828) and that they are "of divine right" (*Code of Canon Law* can. 329). This is, they are not of papal right; the pope cannot suppress them, since they are as much part and parcel of the divinely appointed structure of the Church as he is ... The Vatican Council stands for a condemnation of papalism as much as of episcopalism. Actually it brands both doctrines as erroneous (Ratzinger 1963, 40, 44).

There are times when all other means at the lower levels have been exhausted, when the center of the global church has to intervene in disputes between churches or in difficult, serious, and seemingly deviant situations in which churches, groups, individuals find themselves. When this happens, the center should not act alone, but with the consensus of the local church or churches, and its decisions should follow the pattern set by the first council of Jerusalem (Acts 15:5-29). Sobrino puts the role of the center in a very concise, but meaningful way, "providing leadership, expression and a platform of action for the Church as a whole" (Sobrino 1984, 103).

The center of the global church ought to be accountable not only to the Word of God, but also to the churches gathered in councils, synods, to the episcopal conferences which are responsible for the gospel and for the church in a particular territory. The center has a tremendous responsibility in its role and functions. It touches the lives of millions of people, and binds their consciences in the name of Christ. It ought to be helped by people at various levels, including that of the faithful, who are co-responsible in the fulfillment of its mission. McBrien states this point as follows:

> Neither does the Church have an agency committed to supervising the collective operations of the whole ecclesial machinery. Decisions affecting large numbers of people and large amounts of money are made day after day, at international, national and diocesan levels . . . and the rank-and-file membership of the Church have no institutional recourse against those decisions (McBrien 1973, 89).

Rahner proposes an episcopal advisory body to the pope, which would substitute for the college of cardinals, becoming, in his words

> an important and useful institution. It prevents a false perspective, the impression that the life-streams of the Church ran merely from the head to the members, as if the supreme, officially constituted government of the Church were always also the sole point at which the Spirit of the Church could enter with his new charismatic impulses (Rahner 1965, 70).

The spirit and praxis of the center of the global church should be adopted by all other centers of the church. In this way, Boff says:

> The specific function of the hierarchy is not accumulation but integration, making way for unity and harmony among the various services so that any single one does not trip up, drown out, or downplay another . . . The hierarchy does not exist to subordinate, but rather to nourish the spirit of fraternity and unity. This charism of unity implies all other charisms, such as dialogue, patience, listening, serenity, knowledge of the human heart with its desire for power and self-affirmation. This hierarchical function is carried out by the coordination of a local ecclesial community, by the bishop in his diocese, and by the Pope in the universal church (1985, 164).

This type of center, acting with the style and characteristics mentioned above, would not only be more in keeping with the gospel vision of authority, but would be much more acceptable to the members of the church, and even by members of other denominations, who often recognize the necessity and the usefulness of such a focal point in the church.

Relationship of the Local Church with the Rest of the World

God's mission in the universe has many agents: the Catholic Church, other Christian denominations and religions, all sorts of humanistic groups, systems which run the affairs of the human family of God. How should the global church relate with all these fellow agents of God's mission? I feel that two words would epitomize this relationship: *dialogue* and *cooperation*.

The global church must *dialogue* with all other agents of God's mission. The purpose of this dialogue is manifold. Dialogue helps all to engage in the discovery of the way of God in history for the concrete and yet ever-changing situations of life. God acts in the whole universe and in every single corner of our planet. God's action is not limited by rules, by patterns, by tradition. There is a style of God's operations which is traceable in the holy writings and in the history of humanity. But that style is capable of producing unlimited actions, unexpected actions, ever-new manifestations of God. God's actions in the universe and in each person cannot be predicted, cannot be straitjacketed by humans. How are we Christians going to keep up with a God who surprises us constantly, who is as old as eternity and as new as any new day, or hour, or any birth? Can any one group on earth claim to have a full knowledge of the universe and its creator? Can any one religion assert to know the fullness of God's revelation and love? Can any one Christian denomination profess the complete ownership of Christ and of the Spirit?

Another purpose of dialogue is to discover the riches of other traditions. All creatures, groups, religions and agencies of God's mission on earth need to dialogue to discover the riches of each other, to explore the mystery of the other, to perceive more clearly the gifts bestowed upon one another by God, to learn from each other. God has blessed all peoples, all cultures, all religions, and God's blessings translate into giftedness, into charisms of beauty and spiritual wealth. In a report from the Asian churches at the fifth international conference of the EATWOT, we read:

> Asian Christian Theology should enter into dialogue with other faiths in order to discover and activate the liberating factors they contain, and to discover new insights into its own biblical tradition that may come from encounters with these other age-old religions (Fabella and Torres 1983, 76).

A third purpose for this dialogue is to be able to discern together the signs of God's times. There are so many changes taking place in society, brought about by scientific research, by an ever-perfected technology, by discoveries and inventions, which touch the core of the microcosms as well as of the macrocosms. Humanity has been given the possibility of a new era for all, or of total destruction of life. Vatican II said: "The whole human race faces a moment of supreme crisis in its advance towards maturity" (G.S. 77). And the bishops of the United States declared in their 1983 pastoral letter on peace: "The crisis of which we speak arises from this fact: nuclear war threatens the existence of our planet: this is a more menacing threat than any the world has known." Almost limitless opportunities, as well as the deadliest challenges, face us all. How are we going to discern which way to go? How are we—creatures, groups, religions—going to keep up with all these new scientific and societal changes? How are we going to discern our call in such a confused world, among so many contradictory positions? Dialogue will certainly be one of the surest means to achieve this discernment.

A second activity which will characterize the relationship between the global church and others is *collaboration.* This collaboration begins within the religious realm where many expressions of religiosity can be shared, as Pope John Paul II has frequently shown us in participating in prayer serv- ices with other Christian denominations, with Jews, and with other relig- ions. To express together faith in the same God, to verbalize the religious hopes and concerns for humanity in joint prayers, to celebrate, with rituals and symbols acceptable to all, the events of the human family and of life on earth, should become more common. People who believe in God, who depend on the power of prayer, who strive to live according to religious and ethical principles, should show the world that their beliefs are higher than the barriers which divide them, and should offer a common front of religiosity to counteract a materialist world.

Cooperation must extend to an even deeper, more practical, and broader scale in the response which believers give to the needs of humanity and of the cosmos. As mentioned before, humanity may be on the threshold of a new era, but also at the verge of self-annihilation. The potential for both is enormous. Only in faith can we affirm that the life of the human family of God will continue on earth, in spite of all the threats to it. And yet, what kind of life? Even a quick and very superficial look at the situation of human life on earth will suffice to depict a picture of horror: lack of fulfillment of the most basic needs of people, persecution, oppression, tor- ture, air and water pollution, squandering of the earth's resources, drugs, alcoholism and desperation.

How are believers going to respond to all these needs and situations of peoples? Or change the deterioration of life for countless people and for the earth itself? Or have an impact on the course of world affairs so that God's will is respected and followed? Can any one religion ever dare hope to work alone in the resolution of all these problems which besiege human- ity? Or even make any noticeable impact on the correction of the evils of the world, and in the promotion of love, justice and life on earth? Or would believers not have a better chance for impacting the affairs of humanity when together they address them, together they work to change them, together they promote what they believe and what they stand for? The promotion of God's kingdom on earth would certainly be enhanced if all believers engaged in common projects, spoke with one voice, took joint stances on issues which they believe in and consider important.

METHOD OF THEOLOGY

The global church is more and more developing an *inductive* method of theologizing (Schreiter 1985, 1-38). In this method, the process of theologizing starts from the realities which surround the church. In addition, since we live in a global era, world realities must also be considered by local churches. Whether a purely local or a global trend, in this more inductive approach, situations are analyzed by using the tools of social sciences. By shining on empirical evidence the light of the scriptures and of the living tradition of the Christian community, the community is led to appropriate actions to correct what is not gospelled and to deepen what has been gospelled.

Vatican II was certainly influenced by this method, especially in the formulation of those documents which have a greater pastoral relevance. Synods of bishops always have begun their work with the description of the concrete situations of the topic under consideration. The pastoral letters of episcopal conferences throughout the world follow the same pattern. This method is accepted almost unanimously by third-world theologians, and it is becoming more acceptable to Western theologians as well.

The centrality of the poor in this new method is a key factor. Sergio Torres develops this in "The Irruption of the Third World: A Challenge to Theology" (Fabella and Torres 1983, 3-15). The most revealing phenomenon in the formulation of this theology from the poor is the rediscovery of the Bible as central to life and reflection:

When they open the Bible, the poor want to find there the things of life, and in life they want to find the things of the Bible. Understanding the Bible as a critical mirror of reality awakens a sense of inquiry in the people (Santa Ana 1979, 121).

The Global Church, A Gift of the Poor

I have briefly developed some major characteristics of the emerging global church. I wish now to pinpoint its birthplace. This church has been inspired by the Spirit of the Lord, and its origin is in the local churches of the southern hemisphere. The statement may appear the fruit of an over-enthusiastic missionary zeal. But in reality the majority of the theologians recognize the truth of the statement. In this connection, suffice it to quote from J. B. Metz, who states:

We can see with certainty that this Second Reformation would come neither from Wittenberg, nor from Rome. It would in no way come upon us from out of Christian-Western Europe; instead it will come out of the liberation Christianity of the poor churches of this world. Yet what do these churches really mean to us, these churches in which, tenaciously and not without great difficulties, a new Christian experience of freedom is beginning to prevail? ... Do they truly represent for us a providential situation in which grace is coming to us all? Are they for us the church of a Catholic Reformation? ... I see this hour of reformation emerging from Catholicism and for its way of uniting the freedom of the gospel with the desire of humanity for liberation: it is emerging within the poor churches. Of course, everything will depend on whether Catholicism in the wealthy countries of the world is prepared to recognize the providential mission of the poor churches for the universal Church, and ultimately for the whole of Christianity, and is ready to allow into the heart of the universal Church the forward thrust of this understanding of freedom (1981, 59,78).

The seeds of this emerging church were sown by the Spirit of Christ in the poor churches of the South. Under the Spirit's guidance, the poor developed those seeds, and gave birth to this emerging church, which is most visible in the small Christian communities, but which is beginning to penetrate the larger communities of Catholics throughout the world.

PASTORAL CONSEQUENCES FOR THIRD-WORLD CHURCHES

The thesis of this chapter is that a global church is emerging from third-world churches and that it is a gift to the other churches. In order to fully develop this type of church and to see that the gift reaches its maturity, these churches have a hard task in front of them—a task which they have to fulfil in order to be faithful to the call of the Lord and to their responsibility to other churches.

Being and Acting as True Local Churches

Third-world churches should propose this new vision of church as the one most suited to themselves, and this vision should become the norm in their life and activities. If it is true that the global church is a gift from the churches in the South to sister churches of the North, then these churches should be proud of becoming pioneers in this movement, and take seriously the transformation of themselves into fully local churches.

The global church should be visible not only in small faith communities, but in the "official" churches of the South. The times are propitious. The majority of the religious leaders of these churches are local, the call for indigenization is raised from all corners of the world. To settle for less is to turn a deaf ear to the voice of the Spirit. It could also mean a deadly blow to the aspirations of the members of all churches for a Christianity which is culturally meaningful to them.

Confirming and Strengthening Efforts Already Made

These churches should consolidate all the efforts made by theologians, artists, and musicians to inculturate the church in their lands. Moreover, they should generate new enthusiasm among their members for the continuation of efforts in the same direction. The enthusiasm generated by the council, by Pope Paul VI in Kampala and by Pope John Paul II in his many visits to all the churches, should receive a new boost from these favorable circumstances. New waves of activities promoting inculturation in every church should follow as a consequence.

All Catholic universities, institutes of higher learning and pastoral renewal centers should be stimulated to research and to experiment on different ways of theologizing, of worshiping, and of catechizing. These institutions should become the promoters of indigenization in the church, not in isolation from, but in union with, the people of God, using the peoples' experiences as the basis for their reflections and experimentation.

Local Liturgy

All third-world churches should study the possibility of Asian, Latin American, and African liturgies and request the Holy See to begin the study and the experiments for its formulation and implementation. In light of the recent permission granted by the Holy See to black Catholics of Brazil for Afro-Brazilian rite, this proposal does not seem farfetched:

> In 1986 the Commission of Black Religious Priests [COBB] and Seminarians of Rio de Janeiro, sent a letter to the Vatican requesting the creation of the Afro-Brazilian Catholic Rite. In a surprise move, last February [April 1990], the Vatican allowed the COBB to start the official paperwork for initiating the rite (Serbin 1990, 8).

Given that the number of black Catholics in Brazil is much lower than the number of Catholics in all third-world churches, and, even more, given the importance of Brazil in the future of the church, one can easily see the possibilities if such proposals are made widely, especially if positive answers are given by the Holy See.

The liturgy is the highest expression of the faith and the life of the community. Without an inculturated liturgy there cannot be real life and celebration in the community. It seems that this development could become the first and the rallying point for making the churches in the South true local churches and for these to begin to feel and operate as such.

Ministry in the Churches of the South

Another area for special consideration of the churches of the South is the one on ministry. This is another aspect of the life of the church which has been developed in different ways by these churches, and whose development must be increased and the gains consolidated. The whole issue has to be considered in light of several variables: (1) the increase of Catholics in the South; (2) the needs of individuals and communities, with special emphasis on sacramental needs; (3) the fast decline of the expatriates remaining for a lifetime; and (4) the pattern of growth of vocations in these churches.

It is true that vocations to the priestly, religious, and lay ministries are increasing in the southern hemisphere. But, because of the exigencies of modern life and the increase of the Catholic population, ordained ministers are scarcely able to cope with present demands. Future demands, which will be made upon them by the fast-changing situations of the countries of the South make the picture even bleaker.

One of the most serious consequences will be the inability of many communities to celebrate the eucharist on Sundays and days of obligation. This is due primarily to the canonical regulations, such as celibacy, imposed on all ordained ministers. For as long as the ordained ministry is open only to celibate males and for as long as the eucharist can be celebrated only by them, the situation will not change. Inevitably, it will get much worse.

Everybody agrees on the centrality of the eucharist in the life of individuals and of communities and on the need for a Christian community to celebrate it. Vatican II taught that "really sharing of the body of the Lord in the breaking of the eucharistic bread, we are taken into communion with Him and with one another" (L.G. 7).

Following such words, the Congregation on Divine Worship in its instruction *Eucharisticum Mysterium* of May 26, 1967 could write:

> The aim is to help the faithful to realize that the celebration of the Eucharist is the true center of the whole Christian life, both for the universal Church and for the local congregation of that Church.

Pope John Paul II could not have been more specific on this point. In a 1982 talk to members of the Nocturnal Eucharistic Adoration in Madrid, he stated:

> Our faith teaches us that the Holy Eucharist constitutes the greatest gift which Christ has offered and permanently offers to his spouse. It is at the root and it is the summit of Christian life and of all the Church's activities. It is our greatest treasure which contains "all of the spiritual good of the Church."

Third-world churches should take seriously these and similar statements. In their light one must consider unacceptable the situation of countless communities without the eucharist. With love and courage, these churches would be right to propose solutions which allow their communities to have what is necessary to remain Catholic. If providing the celebration of the eucharist to all baptized and responding adequately to the needs of individuals and communities requires changes in structures of the ordained ministry, these changes should be implemented. It may also show a need to create new ministries or to reshape old ones. Churches should be able to discuss all these and other alternatives and put into practice those solutions which seem most satisfactory. In this search they should be led by their love for their flocks, mindful of the words of Jesus: "What father among you would hand his son a stone when he asks for bread?" (Lk. 11:11).

Formation of Ministers

The preparation of ministers for the Christian communities is another central issue for the churches of the South. Let us consider first the formation of ordained ministers. These churches are blessed with countless vocations to the priesthood. All seminaries are full; more seminaries are being built; existing ones are being expanded. But a question is being asked everywhere: What kind of preparation do these men receive? How can a true and integral formation take place when the qualified staff is not sufficient and when there are too many students in classes or for spiritual direction? Will these seminaries be forced to offer mass formation? Will this formation lead to serious consequences in the future, as it has happened in the North, which also once enjoyed an abundance of vocations but could only provide mass formation?

Pope John Paul II has shown some preoccupation with this problem. In his address to the Bishops of Kenya at the end of their visit to him in 1988, he observed:

> Your seminaries and religious houses of formation are full . . . [This] calls for attention and adequate policies on your part and on the part of the religious congregations regarding the selection and formation of candidates . . . Priests will be properly equipped for their ministries if your seminaries offer a complete spiritual, intellectual and human formation.

And in 1989 the pope took advantage of his World Mission Day Message to insist on the same topic:

> In this message, I wish to stress especially the necessity and value of the presense of autochthonous clergy in the young Christian com-

munities ... Whoever is in charge of the mission must be primarily concerned about good formation of the indigenous clergy, in which rest the greatest hopes of the new Christian communities.

The Congregation for the Evangelization of Peoples has organized seminars for rectors and spiritual directors of diocesan and national seminaries, to conscientize them to the need for a holistic formation of the candidates and to promote greater participation of the faculty in the process of formation. This is a good beginning. But the churches of the South must strengthen such beginnings and ensure that one of the greatest gifts of God does not become a nightmare for them in the future.

There is an aspect of this situation which provides serious questions to the churches. By concentrating most financial resources and the best personnel on the formation of ordained ministers, is there not a danger of neglecting other ministries, especially those of the laity, which the Spirit has also stirred up in these churches and which have proven to be so successful? Would it not be more appropriate to give a solid formation to such other ministers in their base communities? Should the formation of all candidates, both for traditional and non-traditional ministries, be given to them together? If this is done, when they work together in the future, they may be more attuned to each other. I am not suggesting that the *same* formation be given to all, but that *some* formation be given *jointly* to all those who are called to be ministers in the same communities.

The Role of Women in Ministry

The role of women must be kept in mind when we discuss ministries. For the moment all ordained ministers are male, and most other officially recognized ministries are performed by men. Yet the bulk of our congregations and much of the work in them is done by women. So what future is there for women in the ministry of the church? I know of a center in Africa which prepares women catechists. It has a hard time placing graduates because they are not hired by parish priests. Will the churches of the South continue to give women the least recognition and keep them out of decision-making positions?

The churches of the South, I believe, have been chosen by the Spirit of the Lord to give birth to all sorts of ministries. They have experienced their vitality and their usefulness. They must continue to promote all these ministries for their own good and for their mission in the world.

CONCLUSION

In this chapter I have offered reflections on the church. The church in these pages has been discussed primarily as a historical, rather than divine, institution. The divine aspect of the church, nevertheless, I recognize as God's own work. That work is ceaselessly dazzling with mystery and beauty. The historical side of the church is accepted as the fruit of human endeavor.

Though at present several models of church exist within the Catholic Church, my experience tells me that by and large the church exists in the world and operates as a Western institution. This Western church has its own style of relating with churches established in non-Western cultures, with all other religions and groups existing in the world, and its center exercises authority and power over all affairs of the church.

Since the realities of the world and of the church have changed considerably from the time this church emerged, it seems logical that a different type of church be proposed, one which will be more in keeping with multicultural realities. I sketched the main elements of this emerging church, which I have called global church. Elements of it can be found in Vatican II. They are being developed more and more by theologians and episcopal conferences throughout the world. It seems to me that this new vision of the church will not only serve better the needs of its members and of communities, but it will also be a better sign for the rest of the world as it moves rapidly towards a shared global existence.

At the conclusion of this chapter I wish to remind myself and readers that when Catholics speak of the church, they speak of *their* church. It is love that prompts me to write about it. And when we see the need for changes, love must direct us in the search to implement them. What I hope we want is to see that the divine beauty of our mother is not only inward, but external, so that it is as beautiful in its historical countenance, as it is in its divine reality.

4

UNDERSTANDING AND STRATEGIES OF MISSION

In recent years, a great deal has been written about the mission of the church in the world. At Vatican II the church as a whole reflected on its mission and formulated its theory of mission in two major documents: *Ad Gentes* and *Gaudium et Spes*. Subsequent synods on evangelization, on catechesis, on the family, and on the laity have stressed the importance of mission as a whole or for specific areas of the life of the church, and for particular groups of the church's membership.

The encyclical letter *Redemptoris Missio* has offered the latest official teaching of the church on *missio ad gentes*. Its relevant points will be quoted in this chapter to highlight the various understandings of mission and their respective strategies. Missionaries themselves have become more reflective about their mission, and have expressed their views in many articles, essays, and books. As a result of all these reflections, experiences, and documents, the church at present possesses a great wealth of literature which deals with mission, not only in the abstract but also in the concrete situations in which mission is carried out, and by people who are the agents of this mission, be they bishops, priests, religious, or laity, whether full-time, part-time, or even short-term agents of mission.

In this chapter, I will briefly review the more significant understandings of mission, and its more common strategies, as they are viewed and practiced by those members of the church who have dedicated themselves to mission, or as they are contained in the official documents of the church. In reviewing them, I will try briefly to describe each understanding of mission, the socio-cultural and religious background which gave origin to them, the biblical and theological insights on which they are based, and the practices which they propose and are carried out by their proponents.

This chapter discusses the various models of mission which are presently operative in the church and shows how cross-cultural mission can be lived more harmoniously with people who may have a different model of mission.

MISSION AS TRADITIONALLY UNDERSTOOD

Mission in its traditional dress included going to non-Christian lands to convert their inhabitants to Christianity by preaching the gospel, celebrating the sacraments, works of charity, relief, education, and development, and implanting the church as it exists in the Western world.

Socio-Cultural-Religious Background

This understanding of mission originated in the Western world. The Western countries were Christian. Most of the people were baptized and received the sacraments of the church, and they considered their culture and their religion superior to any other culture and religion. Proponents of this model of mission generally consider their church the only, or primary, source of salvation for humankind. So they feel the need to go where the church does not exist, and establish it, with all its Western features, in order to offer salvation to the others.

Biblical Basis

The proponents of this model of mission offer many biblical texts to support it and confirm it. Actually the strongest support for this understanding of mission is the great commission of the Lord to the disciples. Matthew expresses it this way:

> Full authority has been given to me, both in heaven and on earth: go, therefore, and make disciples of all nations. Baptize them in the name of the Father, and of the Son, and of the Holy Spirit. Teach them to carry out everything I have commanded you. And know that I am with you always, until the end of the world (Mt. 28:18-20).

Other texts used by the proponents of the traditional understanding of mission are: Mark 16:15-18; Acts 2:37-39, 10:39-43, 13:32-33, 38-40; Romans 3:21-26; Colossians 1:12-20.

The whole missionary thrust to both Jews and gentiles of the primitive church, contained in the Acts of the Apostles, is also a strong biblical foundation for this mission. All these texts and others, which contain a similar message, have a deep impact on the agents of this mission, and they constitute the deepest and most pervasive motivation for that mission, a motivation which pushes them to acts of heroism, as the history of mission testifies.

Theological Assumptions

Relying heavily on this scriptural basis, the proponents of this model of mission developed a theological awareness which would support it and make it plausible to the members of the church. I will try to sketch the major theological assumptions very briefly and schematically.

Human beings, in this view of reality, live at two distinct levels: the natural and the supernatural. At the natural level of existence, people know God, love God, relate with God, in a human way, with their human faculties, but they are not able to obtain eternal salvation, which comes only at the supernatural level. At that supernatural level, people know God through faith, love God through a love which is a supernatural gift, please God, and can attain eternal salvation in and through Jesus.

Human beings can move to the supernatural order only if they hear, through the preaching of others, about that possibility offered by Jesus, if they believe in that Jesus, and turn their lives over to him through baptism, and if they are able to live at that level with the help of the sacraments.

Since the church alone has that faith, and is the custodian and the dispenser of the sacraments, the church is a necessary means of salvation. "It is necessary to keep these two truths together, namely the real possibility of salvation in Christ for all mankind and the necessity of the Church for salvation" (R.M. 9; see also 20).

To live at that level, one has to possess the true faith, and act according to the true norms of conduct, which only the church through its leaders can ensure, teach, and promote. The church, then, is not only necessary to achieve salvation, but also to bring it to completion in the next world. The church provides salvation, and the church maintains salvation.

The sacraments of the church are another very important aspect of this model of mission. Through baptism, one enters into the supernatural life, and with the other sacraments one supports and develops that life, or restores it, if and when it is broken. And so the process of sacramentalization acquires a very prominent role in this type of mission, greater than many other activities of the church (R.M. 46-47).

The world is unredeemed and it exists outside the church. It is through its mission that the church brings redemption to the world. The world, then, is the field of the church's mission. Once the church is co-extensive with the world, the mission of the church could come to an end. For as long as there is some area, someone outside the church, the mission of the church has not yet come to an end. Once the world is churched, then, redemption and salvation will be available and possible for all.

Since the mission of the church deals with its implantation and expansion, it is imperative that the center of the church be in full charge of it. That is the reason for the center having one of its congregations responsible for that mission, which came to be referred to as missions. The local churches, all the other bishops, are not included in this important activity of the church. They are not part of the enterprise. Those involved in missions come under the Roman Congregation charged with this task, are not answerable to anybody else, do not receive orders from anybody else. Policies, strategies, decisions—all are made by the congregation which is solely responsible for missions. Even those who, like the pontifical mission agencies, cooperate with missions come under its jurisdiction.

Mission awareness and mission cooperation are understood in terms of becoming aware of the number of people who are not yet churched, and of cooperating with missionaries through prayer, sacrifices, and donations, so that they may reach every creature on earth and offer them the possibility of salvation. Within this understanding of mission, then, only ordained and religious personnel can fully be missionaries: others can support the work of missionaries, but they remain at the periphery of mission, as helpers.

Strategies of Mission

By *strategies* here I mean activities that are considered very important by each model of mission. In the traditional model of mission the following strategies emerged in order of priorities. To send missionaries throughout the whole world is the first strategy (R.M. 32, 65). Since faith and the reception of the sacraments depend on hearing the good news, it is imperative that missionaries be sent to preach it, and make available to listeners all that is necessary for salvation, through the specific activity of the church called mission *ad gentes*, "to the nations" (R.M. 34). Missionaries acquire an aura of greatness, of heroism; they command respect and veneration from the other members of the church; they are exalted above any other group in the church.

Following the biblical texts and the theological principles which support this understanding of mission, the second strategy and the first duty of missionaries is to preach, to announce the good news (R.M. 44-45). Evangelization in its strictest sense as proclamation of the gospel is the number one activity of missionaries. No one can ever be considered a missionary without having performed this task. Many times missionaries, who are involved in other activities, such as education, development, work of justice, are asked when they will start doing the real work of the missionary, meaning direct evangelization. The literal interpretation of the text of Paul haunts these missionaries all the time: "Woe to me if I do not evangelize" (1 Cor. 9:16).

The third most important strategy of this model of mission is the implantation of the church (R.M. 48-49). I use the word "implantation" purposely to contrast it with inculturation of the church. Missionaries know the church as it is experienced in their own culture and country. And they establish it, wherever they go, with exactly the same features. The church established by them looks, acts, celebrates, is run in exactly the same way as the church in their homeland. Since the church is understood as the necessary means of salvation, it is imperative for missionaries to set it up as soon as possible. Thus the Western church is established all over, is the same all over, and its implantation is one of the greatest joys of missionaries.

Once the church has been established, and some people have been evangelized and baptized, then the fourth important strategy of mission is sacramentalization. Preparation for the reception of the sacraments, even if it meant memorization of the catechism, celebration of the sacraments, even if it meant just distribution of them in a rather mechanical way, occupied much of the time and efforts of missionaries. Backed by their theology of salvation and Christian life, missionaries saw this ministry as essential for the life and growth of converts. And so they dedicated much time to it, much energy and planning. Thus preaching the good news and sacramentalization are considered the two arms of evangelization.

What about all the other activities in which missionaries are involved, such as education, health services, works of charity and relief, schemes of development? (R.M. 58-60). These are part of mission as traditionally understood, but they are considered pre-evangelization. Their importance and their relevance is derived from their influence on evangelization. To the extent that these strategies are conducive to evangelization, to the possibility of conversion, and provide a chance for preaching the good news, they are considered more or less important and urgent. Catholic schools, hospitals, maternities, works of charity and relief, and plans for development have always been among the best, highly esteemed by the people and their leaders, and command the respect of all. But in the mind of missionaries who follow this model of mission, these activities are really successful when they provide an opportunity for the good news to be heard, for conversion to take place, and membership in the community of believers to be available to the people. No missionary ever disputes or expresses doubts about these activities, but these activities are only preparatory to the *real* evangelization. The question which is very frequently asked of those missionaries involved in such activities is: How many converts did you have this year? That is the real sign of the usefulness and acceptability of pre-evangelization activities. Their importance is weighed against the chances they offer to approach people and expose them to the good news and to the community of believers, not on whether their services are professionally reliable and appreciated by recipients. The importance of the intrinsic goals of these activities is not denied, but it is matched against the chances of conversion they offer.

Since the major activities of this type of mission revolve around preaching and administering the sacraments, and only peripherally doing other things, most missionaries are ordained priests or religious. Real missionaries are the ordained ministers: all the others are helpers of the actual minister. The laity is totally absent, or it has few representatives (like doctors), who are considered more as professionals than as missionaries. Missionaries usually belong to a religious congregation, which solely has the right to be in a given territory, to operate and to evangelize. Nobody else can set foot in that territory, or claim any jurisdiction and right over it. All activities performed are patterned after the ones of the mother or sending church. The church established abroad, the liturgy celebrated there, the religious life developed there, are all a replica of the sending church. Books and subsidies for evangelization come from the same sending church. So missionaries do not feel a great need to study deeply the cultures of the peoples, their religious expressions, their ways of celebration, their rites. Study they do, but more as an anthropological pursuit or a personal drive than the need to know these deep cultural expressions of the people, in order to gear their activities in accordance. And so the missionary churches witness the implantation of all the associations, groups, movements proper to the sending church. One has only to set foot in a missionary station, ask the Christian names of some of the people around the church, look at the associations in existence there, to discover immediately the nationality of the missionaries who operate in that area. This is not said as a criticism of these missioners. This is a reality which accompanies the traditional model of mission, and flows as a natural consequence from the theological principles on which this model of mission is based.

MISSION AS LIBERATION

Mission is helping people who are unjustly treated, persecuted, oppressed by internal and external forces, to liberate themselves, to experience the liberation, the salvation, and redemption brought to all by Christ. Since nobody can truly experience salvation and redemption unless they are totally free from enslaving forces, mission is the means to help people achieve this liberation and redemption which is given by God in Christ. Without this experience in our life, the liberation of Christ remains an illusion. Only through mission as liberation can the redemption and salvation of Christ be effective in people's lives and be meaningful in their existence.

Socio-Cultural-Religious Background

Mission as liberation is experienced and developed by Christians who live in situations of total, or very serious, oppression and injustice. Christians in South Africa, in Latin America, and in other parts of the world, who live under oppression and in situations of degrading poverty, feel that they cannot relate well to, and even less practice, the traditional type of mission, which requires bringing to others the fruits of one's Christian culture and religiosity. They feel that they can hardly go around the world and implant a cultural church to which they do not relate well, or preach a liberation and salvation which seemingly they possess because of baptism and yet never experienced in their lives. These Christians feel that, in order for anybody to really enjoy the fruits of Jesus' redemptive act, one has to first experience in one's life the dignity and the freedom which come with that redemption and salvation.

These realities amount to very little in the lives of people if they are not able to experience them, and to rejoice in them. It does not make much sense to go around the world and transplant something which is not appreciated or is even hated. But it does make a lot of sense for these Christians to consider a mission which requires going with people who struggle for liberation in order to make salvation felt in their lives, and struggle alongside them for total liberation.

This type of mission can appeal to all sorts of marginalized people, whatever the cause of their marginalization may be, and they can be attracted to it, and make of it the deepest thrust in their lives.

Biblical Basis

The charter for the proponents of this understanding of mission is the book of Exodus. This book recounts the experience of liberation of the Jewish people, under the divine intervention of Yahweh, through the mediation of Moses and other leaders. The book itself and all the other passages of the Bible which refer to that experience are truly an inspiration to the proponents of this model of mission and become true guidelines for the strategies of this mission.

Other important passages which animate these people are contained in the books of prophets. The prophets experienced the oppression and injustices perpetrated by the powerful and rich over the people, and felt that the people could not perceive Yahweh's liberating freedom under those circumstances. Consequently, they saw their mission as one of liberation through conscientization and empowerment of people. The process of conscientization was made possible by the teachings of the prophets, and the empowerment was based on the power of Yahweh.

A third and most revealing biblical source referred to very often by those who follow this type of mission is Mary's Magnificat. In it, they discover the purpose and style of Yahweh's mission in the world and in history. That mission is one of subverting systems of oppression and injustice, whatever their cause may be, in order to bring about, together with the empowered and conscientized people, the freedom and justice which alone can make the salvation of Yahweh personal, experiential, and true.

A fourth source of biblical enlightenment derives from the clear and unequivocal statement of Jesus about the last judgment of humanity, as recorded especially in Matthew 25:33-46. A mission that dichotomizes spiritual salvation and physical liberation does not have much chance of support in this passage. On the contrary, the proponents say, a mission which promotes integral and holistic salvation stands the chance of approval at that solemn moment for humanity.

These are not the only passages/books referred to in this type of mission, but just a few to show that this mission is deeply rooted in the Bible, takes its inspiration and, to a certain extent, even its modalities from the Bible.

Actually the proponents of this mission look at the way Jesus himself understood his own mission, as recorded in Luke 4:17-21, and how he practiced that mission as recorded in many passages, but especially in John 6, and try to be inspired by it.

Theological Assumptions

Enlightened by the biblical perspectives mentioned above, by the documents of Vatican II, by *Redemptoris Missio*, and the personal experiences of missionaries, the proponents of this understanding of mission take a different route in their theological reflections.

If, in the history of humankind, there were two levels at which people lived, the natural and supernatural, with the coming of Christ and his redemptive act, these were merged. From that point on, people live at the level of friendship with God, brought to all by Christ. The dichotomy, if it existed before Christ, definitely came to an end with his life, death, and resurrection. Christ has obtained God's love for all, and all peoples are redeemed by God in Christ (R.M. 4, 5, 6, 10). God loves us all; God gives us all grace; God brings us all to union with God. Redemption and salvation are the work of God, and their fruits are available to all. "The universality of salvation means that it is granted not only to those who explicitly believe in Christ and have entered the Church. Since salvation is offered to all, it must be made concretely available" (R.M. 10). Mission then is not concerned with bringing salvation to peoples. That is God's concern, and God does not fail in God's plan.

Redemption and salvation are integral and holistic. They are not only spiritual. They touch the whole person, in all its aspects and components— the spiritual, the physical, the psychological—and they transform them into the likeness of Christ. "Jesus came to bring integral salvation, one which embraces the whole person, and all mankind, and opens up the wondrous prospect of divine filiation" (R.M. 11; see also 14). But they extend beyond the human person to penetrate all that surrounds it, the political, the economic, the social, the cultural, and transform these factors into potentials for life, for freedom, and for growth. Persons truly experience redemption and salvation when they are free from personal forces which dehumanize them, do not allow them to grow, to feel loved, to rejoice in freedom, and to live with a dignity worthy of God's children. And people truly experience redemption and salvation when all that surrounds them is not enslaving them, does not interfere with their growth, but actually promotes and sustains it. To say that a person is saved or redeemed because the soul is free from sin and can go to heaven is to reduce redemption and salvation to merely spiritual entities with no regard to the rest of a human person. It is to play in the hands of those who affirm that religion is the opium of the people, because it is mainly, if not exclusively, concerned with the spiritual and with the other life. On the other hand, to state that redemption and salvation touch all the aspects of human beings and change them into subjects and secondary agents of salvation is to make religion an integral part of humanity in all its growth, in all its aspects.

Not only does redemption touch human creatures and all that is around them, but it also affects the whole of creation and the whole environment. The world is graced, the world is redeemed, the "inchoate reality of the kingdom can also be found beyond the confines of the Church among people everywhere" (R.M. 20). But this salvation must be manifested and operative in all the structures of society, in all aspects of earthly life. These structures are truly redeemed, when they are liberating; whereas they are unredeemed, when they are oppressive. Presently the structures of the world are the cause of the most serious violations of freedom, of the deepest and most pervasive oppression in society. While personal sins are to be considered seriously, social sins are more damaging at this time, when humanity has the power to destroy life on earth, when fear dominates all our political life and social relationships, when governments, in so many countries, go unchecked in their activities, and the multinationals make havoc of the world's creatures and riches. The structures which are presently operative in the political, economic, social, military, and ecological aspects of life, very often are oppressive, make very little of the dignity of human creatures, create situations which do not allow people to experience the fullness of salvation. Though the world and all its creatures are redeemed, the possibility of experiencing this liberation is very much reduced and, at times, impossible, due to the structures present in society, which are suffocating freedom and human dignity for the majority of the people of the world.

The relationship between the church and the world is viewed in terms of complementarity, and not opposition. The church is in the world, and is part of the world. The church is not primarily the cause of salvation, but a sign and an instrument of it (R.M. 20).

As a sign, the church stands for all that God wants for the world, for humanity. The church has to signify to, and for the world, the salvation and redemption won for all by God in Christ. In its life, in its structures, in its activities, and in its relationships, the church must shine forth as the community which is free, which respects the dignity of all, and a body whose structures are truly liberating. But since the church is not a perfect community and can become a cause of oppression and of injustice, it too needs to experience deeper redemption, and it should confess its errors and mistakes with candor and honesty.

As an instrument or agent, the church should get involved in all the situations of the world which are unredeemed, in all structures which are oppressive, in all worldly and human affairs which are threatening life or diminishing it, and actively work to modify them, to change them so that they can become life-giving and not life-taking. The church should also join with all the forces of the world which try to promote those conditions of redeemed life, without hesitation, or hypocritical attitudes and dual standards. Church and world are both God's creatures. The church is in the world, part of the world. The church does not have to conquer the world but to help it modify itself so that all that exists can be redeemed and experienced as redeemed.

The real mission of the church, then, is to make sure that it and all other creatures on earth, all other societies, and all their institutions are truly gospelled. They exist, they operate, they influence everything and everybody they touch in ways that are gospelled, that promote life, that eliminate injustices, inequalities, and all that is not life-giving and life-promoting.

The kingdom is very important in this understanding of mission. Kingdom is the whole universe and all its creatures. They are already touched by God in Christ, but need to make it visible (R.M. 12-15). The kingdom is greater than the church, and wider than the church. The kingdom is where God is, where life is, where love is, where justice reigns, where all that exists and operates does so in a gospel manner, with gospel values and in gospel style.

Mission awareness and cooperation means to help Christians become aware of the oppressive forces which enslave people in the world, especially the poor, and call them to get involved in the process of dismantling the oppressive institutions and the process of integral liberation of all, so that all can experience in their lives the salvation brought about by God in Jesus.

Strategies

One important part of mission as liberation is *conscientization*. To conscientize means to help people know and understand what the root causes are of their lack of freedom, lack of justice, of oppression. It is imperative that people are fully aware of the causes that keep them oppressed, unjustly treated, marginalized, and with no rights. The process of conscientization follows the methodology of Paolo Freire in which the people discover, with some external help, these causes as they exist, but above all as they affect the people themselves.

Analysis of the situation is another important aspect of mission. People must reflect on their own realities, on the meaning, or lack of meaning, in their lives, on the effects produced by those realities. Conscientization and analysis are based on at least four elements.

The Bible. Each situation must be looked at and judged in the light of the Bible. To look at the Bible will help the people see whether a similar situation in which they presently live is described in the Bible, how God judged it, and how the people acted on it, under the guidance of Yahweh. The Bible sheds light over the situation, gives meaning to it, offers general orientations on the way the situation can be understood, judged, and reacted to. The Bible does not give answers to present realities, because each era has different realities to contend with, but it does give orientations and the possibility of comparison and consequent judgment.

Social analysis. Social analysis offers a scientific opportunity to look at all concrete aspects of the situations in their historicized manifestations and a greater chance to determine what action should be taken. Social analysis helps to study concrete situations, in all their complexities, with the tools of the social sciences, and to arrive at a sound and scientific understanding of them.

Sacramental catechesis. Preparation for the reception and celebration of the sacraments offers a further opportunity for conscientization. There is a concerted effort made through catechesis to present the sacraments not just as rites neophytes have to go through, but as moments in the believers' lives which make them aware of their dignity, rights, freedom, and how these values can be violated, or taken away altogether. The sacraments enhance the individual's dignity, they confer power to protect and defend it, when it is violated; and they are inserted in the lives of people to make them grow and mature according to God's plan. I remember being in Guatemala a few years ago and attending a confirmation ceremony. The ceremony was performed at the height of the persecution of president Rios Mont. The bishop asked the candidates: "What is confirmation?" Some of them gave the answer in the catechism. But then the bishop asked a more pointed question: "What does confirmation mean to you?" A young man answered: "Confirmation means that I become a full member of the church, with all its rights and responsibilities, and the Spirit is given to me, so that I can stand up for my rights, claim them for me and for all others, fight for them when they are denied to me and to others, and, if necessary, give my life for them." This is sacramental catechesis in terms of conscientization and life.

Empowerment. The fourth important strategy of this model of mission is the empowerment of people. People must rely on the gifts they have received from God, in their own experience. They must nurture hope, based on the God of the Bible who "has shown might with his arm and has confused the proud in their inmost thoughts; has deposed the mighty from their thrones, and has raised the lowly to high places; has given every good thing to the hungry, and has sent the rich away empty" (Lk. 1:51-53). They must become assured that the movement of liberation of God in history cannot be counteracted by anybody. This empowerment gives the chance to people to act, to react, to take initiative for the changes needed to make salvation and redemption a reality in their lives, in the circumstances of their historical existence.

The basis for this empowerment does not come from arms, from prestige, or from political maneuvering, but from faith in the liberating God of history, and from the power contained in the sacraments. This faith resembles that of Mary who claimed that "God has upheld Israel his servant ever mindful of his mercy: even as he promised our fathers, promised Abraham and his descendants forever" (Lk. 1:54-55). And while that faith supports the intellectual struggle of the people, the sacraments give strength to the will of the people. The sacraments become channels of strength, means of support in the struggle for the fulfillment of the dreams of the people.

MISSION AS MUTUALITY

There are millions of Christians in such conscientized churches in the South. In them we see exemplified an emerging example of *mission* as mutuality. Most of the bishops are native, local clergy and religious are becoming more and more numerous, and most of the institutions are already in place. These churches have developed, or are developing, their own theologies and liturgical celebrations. And so they feel that mission within the church can no longer be a one-way flow from the North to the South, from the churches of Europe and North America to those of Africa, Latin America, and Asia. These churches are claiming a voice in that mission, a place in it, a role in it. And so mission is perceived as mutuality of sharing, of learning, of helping, of prodding. Through this mission, all the inculturated churches of the world listen to each other, learn from each other, and complement what they possess with what is offered them. Mission, then, becomes a two-way street, a constant exchange, a perennial learning.

Biblical Basis

The proponents of this understanding of mission take their inspiration from the Acts of the Apostles, especially the first fifteen chapters. In these chapters, there is a kind of model of mission as mutuality. In fact the Christian faith is rooted first in the Jewish tradition and culture, and absorbs from it most of the external religious elements (Acts 1-6). Then, that faith is brought to the gentiles who understand it, and live it out, within their own cultural experience, and give rise to a slightly different version of Christianity (Acts 7-12). A conflict develops between these two nuanced forms of Christianity. The sending community of Jerusalem perceives the differences between these two forms, and claims uniformity in the faith and its expressions. The receiving community of the gentiles claims freedom of expression of their faith. After a lot of controversy, internal fighting, some maneuvering and the guidance of the Holy Spirit, the two different communities of believers come to an understanding of each other, and accept a compromise which saves the unity of the faith, while acknowledging the pluriformity of its expressions (Acts 13-16).

In this process, the receiving community is grateful to the sending community for the faith received, but claims the right and the freedom to respond to that faith in ways that are culturally meaningful to it. And so the whole process is completed. There is a sending community or church, which has understood and practiced the faith within its cultural background; that community goes out to share their inculturated faith with people of other cultures who, in their turn, try to reinculturate it in their own environment. A clash occurs between these two inculturated forms of Christianity; in this process neither form is to impose things on others, or to attempt to determine the form of Christianity to be developed, but each shares in the endeavor to make Christianity relevant to its adherents and learns from the other.

The proponents of this model of mission have truly found in this process, which first took place in the original community of believers, the genuine way of relating between the various communities of believers, and their mission to one another—a mission that, at the beginning, may be a one-way street, but ceases to be so as soon as the receiving community is able to respond to the gift, and make it its own. Then the two communities enter into dialogue with each other, with no distinction and difference, in order to learn from each other, and to perfect their own way of Christianity with that of others, as the book of Acts clearly demonstrates.

Theological Assumptions

The Catholic Church exists in all continents and in most countries of the world. These geographically distinct churches have much in common: actually they have all the essential elements of Catholicity in common. They have the same creed, the same sacraments, the same liturgy, the same authority, the same general discipline, the same Bible, the same ministry. There is unity among these various geographic churches. The constitutive elements of the church are present, the core of beliefs is held in common, the liturgical life is shared, and a common discipline is revered.

As all these geographic churches try to become local churches, by inculturating themselves, a new phenomenon will happen: unity will be complemented by pluriformity. In fact, while the Catholics will still agree on the same fundamental beliefs, on the same constitutive elements of Christian living and worship, nevertheless, due to the inculturation of all these elements in their respective churches, they will understand, live, and celebrate them in ways that are culturally different and with nuances that are culturally acceptable. Thus sharing the basic elements of Catholicity becomes a mission for these Catholics who wish to take their part in the total mission of the church in the world. In fact by sharing these diverse elements with one another, these inculturated churches will enrich and complement each other, and move towards that pleroma of which Paul speaks in Colossians 2:2 and in Ephesians 3:18-19.

As a corollary of the above, many dichotomies existing in the church at present, which we have been criticizing, would be eliminated. The following may help us better to see the changes that will occur when this understanding of mission prevails among the local Catholic churches. We would move:

FROM	TO
mature vs. new churches	local churches
developed vs. developing churches	churches in development
mother vs. daughter churches	sister churches
sending vs. receiving churches	sending and receiving churches
teaching vs. learning churches	teaching and learning churches

The center of the church, at whatever level, is not primarily the place of authority, of power, of control, but of dialogue and empowerment. In *empowerment*, local churches take the process of inculturation seriously and become truly local churches with their own historical identity determined by the cultural background in which they are and operate. They are free to experiment in the areas of theology, liturgy, Christian living, ministries, community, religious life, and all other aspects of Christianity, so that these local churches can best express the faith of their members and become relevant to them. In *dialogue* among local churches there is an open chance to share experiments, theological insights, adaptations, in order to be accountable to each other, to challenge and to enrich one another. Thus mutuality in mission involves mutual transformation and enrichment.

If the sharing is to bring forth experiments and adaptations in a given church which deviate from the essentials of Christianity, other local churches have the right to question them. But the accountability and the calling to task should be done in the name of the gospel and its genuine values. No church should be stopped from initiating experiments, because they are not done anywhere else, or because they are new, or because they deviate from traditional praxis. The criteria for accountability, and especially for punitive action on the part of the universal church against local churches, should be determined only by gospel values and the living tradition of the church.

Mission awareness and mission cooperation are understood in terms of mutuality. Catholics all over should become aware of the various inculturated churches, their uniqueness, their experiments, in order to learn, to be inspired, and to imitate them.

Mission education is understood as reverse mission. People who have been in cross-cultural ministries share with the members of their sending church their experiences of Christian life in other churches, bring to their attention the problems and difficulties of the adopted churches, and try to influence the government policies favorable to the people of the adopted churches, and change those policies that are detrimental. Thus, bonds of friendship will be established between all Catholics and between them and all other peoples. Bridges will be built between cultures, new understandings and insights in the faith will be shared, and mutual assistance will be promoted with a more personal touch than before.

Strategies

Exchange of personnel is the new word for sending people from one church to another (R.M. 64). The so-called missionaries are no longer

Christians who go from the European and North American churches to other churches, but Christians who go from *any* church to another in whatever direction, to help another local church in its needs and demands (R.M. 32, 62). In the future, we will see African Christians ministering in Europe and North America, as well as Catholics from the latter churches going to Africa. And this holds true of all the other churches. This process has already begun, and its growth in the future will be considerable.

Personnel is sent at the discretion of, or at the request and initiative of, the calling church. It is the local church which feels certain needs, and hears certain demands, which it cannot meet, and asks for help from other churches. The call addressed to Paul—"come over to Macedonia"(Acts 16:9)—will be heard anew by the churches, and the answers will be given in the same vein as Paul's.

The function of these cross-cultural personnel is not to bring their own brand of Christianity where they go, but to share with the local Christians as they try to minister according to the local church's policies. In this sharing, first of all they have to listen, to be attentive to the local church, and to try to fit into it as well as they possibly can. But they also have to bring to the attention of the local church the ways of their own sending church, so that mutuality can be implemented. There will no longer be manipulation, but true fellowship and complete sharing in honesty and openness.

The personnel who are blessed with this cross-cultural experience, when they go back home, have the responsibility to bring to the attention of their sending church the riches of the Catholics of their adopted church. Christians all over the world ought to be in contact with their brothers and sisters from other churches, to be inspired by them, to learn from them, and also to challenge them and to be challenged by them.

In this type of mission, there is no longer a large role for lifetime missionaries. Most of the services rendered are for a set period of time and will be discontinued when the need is fulfilled. That is not to say that there will no longer be *any* lifetime missionaries, but that the missionaries' services will be defined as regards time and need.

This type of mission envisages more lay personnel in mission than ordained or religious personnel. In fact, in a mission of mutuality everybody has the right to share. Sharing is the fruit of personal experience of Christianity as well as of knowledge of it. And since lay persons are much more numerous than the clergy or religious and because they all have their own experience of Christianity, and because many of them are also highly educated in the field of religion, they ought to be more numerous in cross-cultural activities as well. In addition to needed personal experience and knowledge of Christianity, lay people bring many helpful skills and professions to mission, which are for the enrichment of local Christians so that they in turn can carry out their own proper mission (R.M. 71-74).

MISSION AS FULFILLMENT

Mission does not exist to destroy what God has done in the world through people's cultures and religions. Rather, it consists in bringing all this to perfection, in and through Christ in an explicit or implicit way. The God who has created all things in and through the Word through the power of the Spirit is the same who has accompanied peoples on their journeys through history, and has sent the Word into the world to redeem it, to complete it, and to bring it to its original intended perfection. The church's mission exists to help this process in all its stages of development.

Scriptural Basis

The most common and basic attitude of Jesus in his mission seems to be supportive of this concept. In fact Jesus did not come to "abolish the law and the prophets, but to bring them to completion" (Mt. 5:17). If Jesus did this in his own culture and religion, can the church not do the same with the cultures and religions of today's world?

"You are the salt of the earth" (Mt. 5:13). Salt is an ingredient which preserves substances and flavors them. And so are Christianity and the church. They are but a minority of the world's population. But they have the power to help preserve values, religions, cultures, and also they can add something unique to what already exists, as does salt when added to a dish.

"You are the light of the world" (Mt. 5:14). Light helps people to see what already exists. Light makes things visible. Christianity and its followers are not the only religious reality in the world. But they can help others see their own realities more clearly, appreciate them in a deeper way, and yet leave them free to pursue and to study their own traditions with the help of that light.

"The kingdom is like the yeast" (Mt. 13:33). The leaven is not the whole mass of flour in the dough. It is but a small element in that mass. But it penetrates into it, it helps it grow, swell, and rise from within. Christianity operates in the same way in regard to other cultures and religions. It penetrates all cultures and all religions through its mission and it helps them to grow, to mature, to rise a little higher, to be pregnant with more and better life. This may not be the way earlier generations of missionaries understood their roles, but this has been one of the results of their activity, a result we are only now beginning to appreciate.

Socio-Cultural-Religious Background

The proponents of the fulfillment model of mission are Christians who live in countries which have very ancient cultures, very rich cultures, and a fully developed religion with its theology, rites, and symbols. These cultures and religions are so rooted in the life and history of the people that they have become the fabric of their entire existence. These cultures and religions have helped their followers for millennia, have brought them where they are at present, and the people feel happy with themselves and their cultural-religious background.

Would mission mean to destroy all this and to substitute with another culture and religion for it? Would these Christians feel the need to deny their past, to condemn it, and to turn to an entirely different way of life and worship? Would they ask their fellow citizens to renounce all the past in order to join Christianity? Or would they look at all that is in their midst as the fruit of God's work in their lives, respect it, accept it, and try to build on it, and grow within it with Christianity acting as light and leaven?

In the past, Christians living in the countries of the great religions used all the strategies of the traditional model of mission to overcome native traditions, but they did not succeed because the type of Christianity offered was so alien that it did not appeal at all. Would the presentation of a Christianity which does not request conversion as the first requisite, but offers a chance for further growth in the native cultures and religions, and also leaves open the possibility of a change of religion within the present cultural and religious background, be more appealing to the people and constitute a valid mission for those churches? The answer to these questions is a positive one for many Christians of China, Japan, Indonesia, and of other countries in similar situations.

Theological Assumptions

The starting point of the proponents of this understanding of mission is the same as that of mission as liberation. God is the one who saves, who redeems. And God extends that redemption and salvation to all peoples, without any distinction (R.M. 55). So mission is not primarily concerned with bringing salvation and redemption.

This salvation and redemption, brought about by God, are normally achieved in and through religions. God "does not fail to make himself present in many ways, not only to individuals but also to entire peoples through their spiritual riches, of which their religions are the main and essential expression" (R.M. 55). Religions are the normal way through which God reaches people and brings them to friendship with God, communicates with them, helps them understand themselves and the realities around them, and helps them live in harmony with God, themselves, and creation. This does not necessarily mean that all religions are the same, but that all religions have the same purpose and perform the same task on earth.

If religions are the normal conduit of God's action on people's life, then religions must be respected, not destroyed. Nobody should destroy what

God has done in and through them. And nobody should condemn what God has used as an instrument for reaching out to people to bring them to growth of life and humanity. All should be concerned about safeguarding religious freedom (R.M. 8).

World religions, then, should not feud with one another or be antagonistic to each other. Rather, they should help each other obtain what they promise and what they work for in the best possible way. There should not be rivalry between religions, but healthy and lively interaction and dialogue (R.M. 29).

The action of the Spirit is stressed in this model of mission. It is only through the power of the Spirit that people are enabled to come to a greater awareness of God's action in their lives, and there can be revealed the total plan of God for humanity in and through Christ (R.M. 21, 22, 28). Since nobody is able to say "Jesus is Lord, except in the Spirit" (1 Cor. 12:3), Christians never cease to hope that the Spirit will reveal this mystery to others, and they do all that is in their power not to impede that revelation. But they are not discouraged when such revelation does not take place, because they know that only the Spirit can offer it, and the Spirit is completely free in bestowing that grace.

Mission awareness and cooperation is primarily a means to let the Christians be aware of the riches and the beauty of the ancient world religions, to learn from them or reclaim through their help some elements which may have been abandoned as a result of the colonial era and, above all, to enkindle the desire for interfaith dialogue and cooperation in projects which promote the kingdom of God on earth.

Strategies

The first strategy is interfaith dialogue. This dialogue is meant to help all world religions to know each other better, to respect one another and most of all to probe together the infinite mystery of God, God's presence and actions in the world, God's new calls to humanity. God is infinite and is revealed in so many different ways, through so many varied channels, as the letter to the Hebrews tells us (Heb. 1:1). To study this mystery together, to reflect on it within the various religious faiths and traditions, to contemplate through the prism of religious beliefs God's manifestations in history, would give members of all religions the best chance to penetrate deeper and deeper into this mystery, and to keep pace with it in its ongoing revelation to humanity (R.M. 56-57).

With interfaith dialogue, there should also be interfaith cooperation. All religions should work together to promote, within their own faith awareness, life in all its manifestations, and those qualities of life which are in keeping with the plan of God for humanity. Presently, humanity faces gigantic and universal problems, as well as new and far-reaching opportunities. Religions should join together to face these problems and provide solutions which their faith and religious beliefs would suggest; and they should also explore together the new horizons and the new frontiers of human development, so that they can truly be God's agents in this world and help humanity move into the future in directions provided by the Spirit of God.

As Christians and all other world religions practice dialogue and interfaith cooperation, they themselves will be enriched, and their members will have a unique opportunity to grow in their respective religious awareness. This growth could lead believers to become better believers who are better acquainted with their own faith and who practice it with deeper conviction and commitment. It could also lead believers to discover or rediscover new religious realities which could enrich them even more. Christians are rediscovering contemplation with the help of the oriental religions. And the followers of Eastern traditions are discovering commitment to social needs through contact with Christians. This dialogue and cooperation may take members to an even greater awareness of each other.

This acceptance of other believers' faith is not so much conversion as it is growth towards a newly discovered religious awareness. If conversion does occur, the members who join another faith ought to be helped so that all the valid religious elements present in their previous faith are kept and are incorporated in the newly discovered faith. What happened at the beginning of Christianity should be repeated in our days. As at the origin of Christianity there were Jewish Christians and gentile Christians, so, at present, there could be Buddhist Christians and Hindu Christians. Christianity would become the apex and the ultimate expression of all religions. And all religions could find in Christianity a home where all their elements which are not in direct contradiction to the gospel would be accepted, respected, welcomed, assimilated, and allowed to inspire Christianity in all its manifestations.

Religious studies of the future should consider the various religious perspectives in order to be holistic. Whatever topic is taken into consideration should be looked at, not only from the Judeo-Christian perspective, but from the perspective of all major religions. Creation, fall, redemption, grace, sacraments, forgiveness, justice, and similar topics should be studied in a holistic way as they are understood by the various religions so that the whole spectrum of beliefs about them may emerge and become familiar to all believers. This approach would provide the opportunity to see the similarities and differences that exist in each topic among the world religions, and thus stimulate the faithful to mutual respect.

MISSION AS RADICAL DISCIPLESHIP

Mission is also living a radical way of life according to the values of the gospel. The most radical values of the gospel, lived without domestication, become the mission of people who "can do no other," who choose it voluntarily, and out of a faith commitment.

Socio-Cultural and Religious Background

This model of mission as radical discipleship is proposed by Christians who live in countries where religious freedom is nonexistent for Christians and many other freedoms are curtailed. Christians who live in some Muslim countries and who are not allowed to preach, or to speak out against injustice or to dialogue with other religions and who are barely tolerated by the people and their governments, feel that they can still remain in such countries and exercise mission in the way which is possible to them. Their only possible mission is the witness of the presence of their own lives lived according to the most radical demands of the gospel. I remember an incident which, at the time it happened, did not make much sense to me, but which has since become symbolic of a ministry of presence. I was going to Africa for the first time. The boat stopped in Aden, and I took the opportunity for a visit to the city. I met a Franciscan who told me that in twenty-seven years of missionary life in Aden, he had not baptized one person. I was stunned. And I asked him: "But, then, what is your mission for?" And he answered me: "My mission is my gospel life without any additions."

There are also some Christians who choose this type of mission out of the conviction that radical discipleship is for them the best way of being in mission. The way they live becomes the best sermon, the most effective catechesis, and the most revolutionizing means of propagating their faith.

Biblical Basis and Theological Assumptions

The biblical texts used by the proponents of mission as fulfillment are also used by the proponents of this type of mission. "You are salt . . . You are light . . . You are leaven."

In addition to those texts, those who follow this model of mission look at the hidden life of Jesus, as described by Luke and Matthew, and they derive great inspiration from it. The mission of Jesus began with conception and ended on Mount Tabor. Most of it was exercised in the hidden life of Nazareth, and only a few years on the roads and in the synagogues of Palestine. If Jesus, the missionary par excellence of the Father to humanity, exercised his mission in this way, why can modern missionaries not do the same and remain true missionaries?

Besides the example of Jesus, there is also that of Mary and Joseph. They too were intrinsically connected with the mission of Jesus—and most of that mission was exercised in the home, in the hidden and radical life of poverty, of sacrifice, of persecution and anonymity.

The mystery of the cross is central to this understanding of mission. The apparent defeat of Jesus on the cross, his complete annihilation, his *kenosis* are the strongest inspiration and the most valid support for the agents of this mission. As the cross was one of the most effective acts of Jesus' mission, so the sacrifices, the humiliations, the lack of freedom, the denial of religious rights, can themselves become a powerful way of mission.

Strategies

Since no other means practiced by other models of mission can be used, either because of circumstances or because of personal choice, and the only possible means is presence and witness, these become the only strategy of mission, or "the only possible way of being a missionary" (R.M. 42). To be present in the most radical way, to live according to the most difficult values of the gospel, to follow Christ humble, persecuted, and crucified, to respond with love to hatred, and to turn the other cheek, is to be in mission, to exercise mission, and to contribute to the mission of the universal church in one of the most hidden and yet very valuable ways. These strategies are based on the conviction that the grain of wheat must die to give life, that the disciple's mission is not different from the master's, and that one's presence and witness are a powerful means for mission.

CONCLUSION

At Vatican II, in subsequent synods of bishops, and more recently with *Redemptoris Missio*, the church has endeavored to reflect on its mission in the world, and it has sketched models of that mission as well as ways to exercise it meaningfully and fruitfully. Christians in mission have made special efforts to reflect on their own experiences in mission and to relate them to the rest of the church's members as part of the ongoing process of conceptualizing what is central to the life and activities of the church—its mission. A kaleidoscopic variety of concepts, models, and practices of mission have emerged in this chapter. Part of the reason for such a variety is the earnestness with which local situations, cultures, and religions were taken into account. Mission is no longer considered an a priori reality, with no linkage with the social realities in which it is exercised, but a response to these realities and challenges (R.M. 32). And since these realities change from place to place, mission also acquires a variety of forms (R.M. 33). As a consequence, mission with all its elements is perceived differently by various groups of people living in different situations, is expressed in a variety of ways, and is practiced with strategies which may even seem to contradict each other.

Mission is so central to the life of the church that the church is missionary by its very nature (A.G. 2); and "in the Church's history, missionary drive has always been a sign of vitality, just as its lessening is a sign of a crisis of faith" (R.M. 2); nevertheless its understanding and practices are manifold and varied. This pluriformity does not destroy its importance for the church, but reinforces it, while giving it greater relevance to the situations in which people find themselves. The knowledge of this pluriform understanding of mission and its many practices will be of great help to Christians involved in mission, as well as a challenge. It will challenge them constantly to review their understanding of mission, so that it will never be taken for granted; it will help them to make their mission more incarnated and meaningful to those whom they serve. People in mission welcome both the challenge and the help, and are looking forward to a new era of the church's mission, and to renewed efforts by all Christians, according to their respective understanding of mission, and the strategies they devise, under the guidance of the Spirit, and the reflections of the community, identified by God's people and accepted by the church's authority.

5

TEAM MINISTRY
IN THE GLOBAL CHURCH

Team ministry in Christianity is as old as the team gathered by Jesus, at least in its embryonic elements, and as recent as the 1970s, when it was being frequently discussed and became an ideal for many women and men who tried to minister together with a distinct style of Christian leadership and service.

In this latter expression team ministry represents a novelty in the church. Some people welcome and cherish it, while others are skeptical about, or even opposed to it. Those who prize it, see in it a more just and Christian way of exercising ministry in the church, and one which offers greater possibility of cooperation among the various ministries which operate in a Christian community. Those who oppose it see in it another post-Vatican II fad, or an attempt on the part of the laity, especially women, to get hold of ministerial power and roles which, they think, are reserved only for some people in the church.

This chapter will present some reflections on team ministry. It will first outline a way of exercising or structuring the exercise of ministry all too common in the church. Then it will attempt a description of team ministry with a short explanation of all its components. It will also offer some reasons for the importance and urgency of developing team ministry. It will propose some crucial consequences for those who wish to attempt team ministry in their respective communities. Finally, possible ways of setting up and running team ministry will be explored.

DEFORMATIONS OF MINISTRY

This way of exercising ministry allows only one minister in the community. He does everything for the community. He celebrates the rites, holds all the power, gives all the orders. Not only does this minister do everything for the community, but also he scarcely allows anybody else to operate in it. When it comes to ministry, he is it. Most of us have had direct experience with this kind of ministry, and we know very well how frequent it still is.

There is also a type of ordained minister who allows a restricted number of other ministers (mainly men), but they must operate under his authority, to the extent that he allows them, and with the style and boundaries that he sets for them. These other ministers are a function of the ordained minister, they do what he cannot do, or does not want to do, or is incapable of doing (though he never says so), but they have no say, no input, no alternatives to offer. They are alter ego of the ordained minister who appoints them and removes them, controls their actions and dictates their behavior.

A less-recognized deformation of Christian ministry occurs when it is professionalized or bureaucratized. Some ordained ministers (possibly many in the churches of the North) set up a system of ministries which parallels those of civil or corporate bureaucracies. In this system there is an organogram which operates like the brain of the system, and spells out clearly who has the supreme authority in the team, how, and to what degree, that authority is shared by the various departments, what is the line of dependence between the departments and subdepartments. Job descriptions are readily available for each of the heads and members, and they define everything from salary to leave, from duties to rights, from maternity leave to paternity benefits. It is against that job description that a person will be evaluated, promoted, fired, penalized, or rewarded. Communication is carried on through memos and notes, with copies to all those senior to the writer and the addressee.

Though such administrative teams are functional and, at times, highly effective from an administrative point of view, one wonders whether there is much room left for the Spirit of God, for the members of the community themselves, or whether the Spirit has been straitjacketed by the structure and the members are victims of modernized oppression.

There are other models of structuring and exercising ministries in the church; but they are variations of, or a combination of, the above.

THE CONCEPT OF TEAM MINISTRY

Team ministry is a way of serving in which all ministers are considered equal. Their charisms are welcomed and appreciated. All share in the decision-making process. All are responsible for the execution of the plans. Each member is accountable to the whole team for their activities.

Team Ministry Is a Way of Service

Each ministry is a service to the community of the believers, and not a privilege or a position of prestige, giving honor and status to the minister.

Service means true concern for those served by the minister, love for them, caring about them, going out to them as much as possible at their level.

Ministers who are servants are concerned about the good of the people and not about reward, recognition, promotion. Nor are they deterred by humiliations, lack of external success, lack of appreciation. Naturally, appreciation and cooperation are welcome, if and when given; but they are of little consequence when not given. In a Christian community, authority and charisms are for service.

This, though, is but one way of service. Team ministry cannot, and should not, be considered, or proposed as the only way of service. It could be argued that, at present, this may be the best way of serving the Christian community. But the Spirit of God can stir up in the community other methods of service now and in the future. And we should be ready to accept other methods which will prove more in keeping with the situations of the community at any given stage of its development.

All Ministers Are Considered Equal

The members of the team are ministers. That is the basic reality on which they are grounded, a reality which recognizes and which prompts them to treat each other as equal, to relate with one another at par, to deal with one another with respect and love. This equality does not deny their various ministries, their different roles, but it highlights their common denominator—the fact that they are all ministers.

Whoever is in charge of the team considers himself or herself as a first among equals and acts as the focal point of the team, a sign of unity among all members, a coordinator and animator of the team's activities. This accepted equality of the team members translates into practice the idea of collegiality of Vatican II and offers a model of collegiality to be studied and followed by team ministers at all levels.

Team ministry stresses a new spirit and a new style of ministry, by giving emphasis to certain values and attitudes which were not important in the past but seem very important at present. Its proponents often express the hope that, if many communities will undertake the experiment, theology regarding ministry and canonical laws which govern it may be changed for the better.

The Charism of All Ministers Is Welcomed and Properly Utilized

Each ministry is based on a charism which is given by the Spirit. That charism is the core and the foundation of ministry, the claim for ministry, the guarantee for some success in ministry. It is a gift, and it is bestowed by the Spirit. It is a grace for the building up of the community. Ministers operate by force of that charism. The official canonical mandate for ministry is only a recognition and acceptance of the charism and not a bestowing of it.

Since all charisms are important gifts, they must be accepted, recognized, appreciated by the team, and allowed to operate freely. The team should be happy at the results, rejoice over the achievements, proud of the success of each of its members. Ministers do not exist because the one who is in authority calls them forth, neither do they operate because they want to. Ministers exist and act in their own right. They do not exist because a benevolent and condescending authority has allowed them to be. Neither do they operate according to the whims of those in authority. In a Christian community, the fullness of ministry comes from the sharing of the charisms of all the members of the team, not from one single minister.

All Team Members Share in the Decision-Making Process

To minister in a pluralistic world and in complex situations requires understanding of differences, adequate planning, and accurate execution. There is a need to listen to the experiences of those ministered to and to study the situations carefully in order to charter an intelligent and meaningful plan of action. Situations have to be diagnosed with sound theological, sociological, and cultural analysis. And resultant decisions have to be made with logical reasoning and accuracy.

The days when one person could make all final decisions alone are over. Decisions which give any hope of successful results have to be made in unison. All team members must bring their expertise, their experiences, their insights, and those of the people whom they serve, into the process of decision-making. To reduce our apostolate to uniformity of activities, to the same humdrum routine day in and day out, is to become stagnant in a society which changes constantly and rapidly. To expect that every decision be made by one person is to lead the apostolate into chaos and ruin, or subject it to dictatorial and blind power.

All Team Members Responsible for Group Decisions

Once the plan of action has been approved and the decisions made and finalized, then each team member must feel responsible for its execution. Members have to go ahead and feel perfectly free to fulfil the decisions according to their own judgment, style of operation, way of acting. Other ministers on the team, especially the head of the team, should not interfere unduly, or try to influence and impose their own ways and means of action.

Team members must be convinced that each person has his or her own methods and style of ministry, common sense, speed, and sense of responsibility. Even if other team members might perform better, they should not interfere to change the agreed plan during its implementation.

Is there, then, any accountability? Is the minister responsible to anyone? Yes, of course.

Each Minister Responsible to the Whole Team

Each member of the team has to give an account of her or his ministry in relation to the team's overall vision. This accountability is not to any individual minister, not even to the one who is the head of the team. In this way, all members keep in mind the general policies and the plan prepared by all members of the team. The team members have the right to question each minister in the light of the above-mentioned criteria. They have the right to critique the way of ministering, to propose alternative ways, and even to demand changes or to pass judgment on the conduct of any of the team members, and to take punitive action whenever the team, as a whole, decides to do so. But suggestions, requests for change, and punitive actions have to be prompted by the fact that a given minister has deviated from the team's vision, policies, plan of action without clear reasons, without sufficient consultation, and not because the minister is not liked by the other ministers, or by the head of the team, or for other reasons which have nothing to do with the team itself, its vision, its plan, or the execution of that plan.

Members Renewed through Prayer, Sharing, and Challenges

Of all the characteristics of team ministry, this is possibly the most difficult to implement, and yet it is also the most important one. In fact any other group of people who work for a goal, or for a company, a school, will have to follow most, if not all, of the procedures mentioned so far. But a team of ministers is a special group of people. These are the ones who have a faith which is the foundation of all they do. They follow a gospel which is spelled out clearly in the teachings of Jesus, and manifested even more clearly in his example. Jesus' teaching and example regarding ministry, and how ministry is conducted in a community, are extremely clear and do not allow for much interpretation. Team members may have a good professional preparation or a long experience in a given type of ministry, which must be respected and treasured. But these people form a team not only to work more effectively, or to minister more fruitfully, but to become better disciples and more dedicated ministers through the contribution of all the members, and the experience of ministry each brings to the team. They need to sustain each other, to support one another, to edify one another, to call forth from each other the best in each, and to challenge the others in truth and charity in the name of gospel values, not of human or personal theories or preferences. A team of ministers is a small faith community which grows, struggles, prays, and shares a life of ministry and the vicissitudes of each person with love and determination.

THE IMPORTANCE OF TEAM MINISTRY

There are many reasons why the idea of team ministry has become so popular recently and has proposed itself to the consideration of the church. I will mention a few of these reasons, and offer a brief description of each.

The New Model of Church Proposed by Vatican II

Vatican II contains a variety of models of church. The one which has all the characteristics of newness, and which immediately captured the attention of many Catholics, is the church as people of God. The people of God are on a journey, and God has endowed them with all the priestly and prophetic powers needed for the journey. During this journey they are called to live as communities of faith, love, and service, to celebrate the Lord's death and resurrection in rites meaningful to the people and to be committed to the building of God's kingdom together with other people on the same journey. They are guided by the Spirit through the signs of God's times, and the members support one another with their example, concern, and love, and are aided by ministers who act according to the charisms received. This help is in the form of service and not domination, of leadership and not power, of assistance and not oppression, of shepherding and not lording it over others. These ministers are themselves a small community, and are invited to serve the larger community as a team. They ought to set an example of how Christian communities live, operate, and serve. Within this model of church, ministry is expanded considerably. It becomes a new reality, and its functions are directed toward helping to build the larger community of believers and, with them and through them, building the kingdom of God.

Vatican II has inspired a type of ministry which is more in keeping with the gospel than with the law, based more on the Spirit than on power and authority, and directed more to the needs of people than the traditions of the community. Vatican II has rooted ministry in history, has pneumaticized it, and has made it available to all who are called. Above all Vatican II has called for a sharing of ministries among God's people, and for a recognition of many types of ministry. Vatican II has brought back ministry to the mainstream of the church's life, recommending plurality of ministries, cooperation among ministers, acceptance of ministries, and proper utilization of ministers for the good of the people and for the growth of the kingdom. This is exactly the concept of ministry proposed and espoused by team ministry.

Needs of People

The needs of people are so many, so varied, so difficult to serve, that only a variety of ministries working together can hope to respond to them in an adequate way.

There are *emotional* needs of people who may be considered normal, or who have serious problems. One has only to set foot in a counseling center to become aware of the enormous number of clients who go for help, for solace, and for some hope of change in behavior.

There are *professional* needs of people who, because of their knowledge, their academic background, require special pastoral care and adequate professional assistance. How many professionals have grown tremendously in one aspect of their personality, and have remained midgets in others! And how many professionals abandon the church because they cannot find adequate spiritual assistance in the regular pastoral work of ministers.

There are *cultural* needs of people who desire to see their cultural values, traditions, way of life mirrored in their religious experiences and in the life of the church. They too necessitate ministers who can help them inculturate faith, religiosity, liturgy, in ways that are meaningful to them—ministers who can bridge the gap between religion and life as it is lived in a particular cultural setting. There are cultural needs stemming from the pluriformity in which we all live. Many Christians, because of the fast changes in society and in the church, live in several worldviews, and are confused, almost lost in a forest of pluriformity which they cannot cope with. They need ministers who can help them make sense of life and feel comfortable with diversity.

There are *ecumenical* and *interreligious* needs, which require the specialized ministry of dialogue and understanding. The scandal of the divisions among Christians and between Christianity and other world religions must come to an end. Members of these religions must be prepared to accept each other, to respect one another, to cooperate in many areas of human living. This is a difficult ministry, but also a very urgent one, and it requires special attention in our pastoral work.

There are needs for *healing.* Many people are hurting badly because they are alienated from the church and society and yet they cry out for help— people like the refugees, orphans, AIDS victims, and homosexuals. They need a ministry of compassion, of co-agonizing, of healing with a depth of sensitivity, which can come only through a charism of the Spirit.

There are needs of *national, international, global* and indeed of *cosmic* nature which are felt by millions of people who are preparing themselves for the global existence of humanity. They feel the necessity of ministers who can walk with them to equip them with proper ethical and religious values for that type of existence.

Faced with these and the many more needs of God's family on earth, how can the church respond with ministries which are both faithful to the gospel and relevant to the people?

The Emergence of the Laity in the Church

Our church, up to a few years ago, counted its educated people primarily among the clergy and religious. The laity, in regard to theological education, were untrained. All of a sudden, lay people are as numerous in seminaries as are the candidates to the priesthood and religious life. They have shown an intense interest in religious matters which translates into attending courses at the academic level, and participating in all sorts of seminars and workshops at the popular level. The thirst for biblical knowledge seems unquenchable, the desire for theological awareness is very deep, and the quest for religious experiences is spreading more rapidly than it can be answered. In the realm of secular knowledge, Catholics in all parts of the world are among the best educated people and hold high positions in the fields of politics, economics, academia, medicine.

When the laity are so well prepared professionally and so desirous of religious awareness, can they be kept apart from involvement in the church? Can they be dismissed as second-class Christians? Can ministers approach them without proper preparation, and serve their needs without consultation with other ministers? The laity are ready to minister, are prepared for ministries, and are gifted with the charisms of the Spirit for ministry. They cannot be left out any longer or be served by just any type of ministry. Only a team approach can welcome them and their charisma and serve their needs.

The New Presence of Women in the Church

Women are emerging in new ways in society. Their presence at all levels of life and activities, their influence in decision-making, their insistence on equal rights and their attitudes in matters of life, war, peace, and the environment are bringing new life and new points of view to society.

In the church, women are more and more claiming their rights as full members. They are, as they have always been, the backbone of the life and activities of the church. But they want to be part of the policy-making and not only to participate in the execution of plans made by males. They are becoming more vocal in claiming the right to determine their own future. They long to bring their own experiences as women to bear on the life of the church, and to let those experiences determine the policies of the church.

The movement of women in the church is probably the most significant contribution to a variety of ministries, to different approaches to ministry, and to different styles in ministry. Women bring dimensions to the ministry which are more in keeping with team ministry and which can truly enhance it in many ways. Actually team ministry has been proposed and practiced by women, first in their own groups and then extended to mixed groups. They are the ones who courageously and patiently try to motivate others to move into such ministry.

THE CHALLENGES OF TEAM MINISTRY

It seems to me that the challenges which emerge from the definition of team ministry for those engaged in it are threefold: theological, psychological, and methodological.

Theological Challenges

In the church, the theological understanding of ministry, in general, has undergone a deep change in the last thirty years. The concept of ordained minister, in particular, has experienced an even greater and deeper metamorphosis.

Ministry used to be understood in terms of ordination and canonical commission. The exercise of ministry was perceived in terms of authority. The real ministers were the ordained priests. They exercised all ministries, and they held all the power in the church. Their word was final, and their decisions irrevocable. Ministry gave them a high status in the eyes of the faithful, and much prestige in society. Accountability was almost nonexistent unless a minister had serious moral failings or grave scandals became public. And, even then, the responsibility was mainly vertical, and seldom rendered horizontally to the people of God as a whole.

The new theological understanding of ministry proposed by team ministry is exactly the opposite. Ministry is a call. The call is based on a charism from the Spirit, either through nature or grace. There are as many ministries as there are charisms. Ministry is related to the needs of the community, and it is exercised as a service. No prestige, no high position, no privilege. All ministers operate by force of their gifts and all should be considered equal. The role of the ordained minister is limited but equally challenging and fulfilling. The ordained minister is the promoter of other ministries, the caller of other ministers, the supporter of other ministers, and the animator and coordinator of ministries in the community. Team ministry promotes a renewed understanding of ministry and challenges all the members to operate according to this spirit—a task very difficult to accomplish and one which requires constant commitment and unselfish determination from all members of the team.

Psychological Challenges

Following the theological understanding of ministry, the consequences for psychological changes are enormous and far-reaching. I have hinted at a few in the course of this chapter. Many more can be deduced from the present team-rooted theological understanding of ministry. Let me mention here two major changes which are probably at the basis of all other psychological changes needed to practice team ministry. One is related to the ordained minister and the other to the other ministers.

The ordained ministers have to change, substantially abandoning any form of superiority complex. They must be convinced that ordination does not give them infallibility or special wisdom making their ideas always the best, their decisions always right, and their directions always correct. They must stop lording it over people and truly start shepherding them as Jesus did and as Peter strongly recommended. They must let go of accumulating offices for themselves and allow others to minister to God's people and with their own ideas and methods.

If ordained ministers have to change in the direction of de-escalating and de-emphasizing their role, other ministers, and especially women ministers, have to change in the direction of escalating and emphasizing their presence, role, and activities. For too long, these ministers have accepted passively, with a submission which has nothing to do with the gospel virtue of patience, a concept of ministry, a style of ministry, and the role of the ordained minister, which are, at times, oppressive and ungospelled. The nonordained ministers have to become more aware of their own roles, and they must claim them with Christian strength and conviction. They are not an appendix to the ordained ministry. They are not puppets in the hands of the ordained minister. They are not simply a help to the ordained minister. They are ministers in their own right. They exercise ministry according to their own call. They deserve to be treated as co-ministers, respected as co-ministers, accepted as co-ministers.

In my description of team ministry, I have referred to changes in the method and style of ministry. I will develop further this aspect of the topic later in the chapter. For the moment the few changes mentioned earlier are sufficient.

CROSS-CULTURAL SITUATIONS AND TEAM MINISTRY

The challenges offered by team ministry to the church in general are even more acute in cross-cultural situations. And yet the necessity for establishing team ministry in those situations is even more crucial than elsewhere. Cross-cultural ministers ought to engage in the establishment of team ministry if they wish to serve effectively in the situations they encounter in their pastoral life. The difficulties should not deter them, but spur them on as they engage in the task of team ministry building.

Most churches in third-world countries still have a large contingent of expatriates who minister on a regular basis as well as a growing number of local ministers. For the sake of clarity and brevity, I will choose Africa as a case study for this part of the chapter. Though there is a lot of good will on both sides, cooperation between local ministers and expatriates is not easy. Many reasons concur to explain this situation—continental differences, cultural differences, colonial past, sense of superiority and of pride, and a desire for identity and authenticity. And yet these people live side by side, work in neighboring parishes, often share the same offices or roles. Failure to constitute themselves as a team where these differences are homogenized and sublimated by the love of God and by the desire to serve the people of God by helping communities grow to full maturity and complete sufficiency will mean disaster for the churches of Africa and of the Third World.

Among the local ministers, tribal differences (or caste, or class differences) still make their influence felt. Among the expatriates, membership in different religious congregations, nationality, and various degrees of education are a hindrance to harmonious and loving ministerial relationships. Ministers should look upon these differences as challenges. If Christian ministers are not able to utilize them in a way that will enrich our ministries, then our Christianity is still very shallow and our ministries are motivated more by self-interest than by the community's growth and welfare.

Most local communities are served by nonordained ministers. These ministers are still the backbone of our church. In the past, without them, very little could have been done to promote the Christian message and to expand the church. At present, without them, even less can be done to boost the life of the communities and to promote integral evangelization. The nonordained ministers in Africa constitute one of the most valid means of evangelization, human promotion, and expansion of the faith.

Catechists form one of the most important ministries. Christian teachers are a presence of knowledge and an example in the schools. Doctors, nurses and medical staff are the visible sign of God's healing power for the sick. Social workers are an expression of the Lord's concern for the qualities of human life. All these people are ministers of God's presence and love in the world. They need to feel part of a team, to be called together for faith experiences, to pray together for strength in their respective ministries, and to be helped in their difficulties. They need to be with other ministers to reshape their vision of ministry, to share their experiences in ministry, to be consoled in their apparent or real failures, and to gain momentum in the exercise of their ministry. In isolation they can experience frustration. While they may be able to continue their *professional* tasks, they may give up their *ministerial* identities. What will happen to the churches of the Third World if these nonordained ministers cannot function as such because they feel marginalized, unwelcomed, barely tolerated, and not supported and treasured? Will Catholic churches lose more and more members to other groups which empower their followers to be authentic and active ministers of God's love in and for the world?

There is a further consideration which manifests another strong need for team ministry in third-world Catholic churches. There are special ministries whom the church condemned in the past and from whose exercise Catholics were barred. These specialists are called by different names in each culture, but all of them, at least in Africa, are healers, reconcilers, medicine persons, and the like. Presently these traditional ministers are being looked upon in a different light, their role and influence on the people are being reconsidered, and their reputation is gradually being reinstated. Catholic communities should not disregard these healers, especially if they become members of the church. They ought to become part of team ministry, and their natural, extranatural or supernatural power be properly used for the comfort and well-being of people. These healers still retain an extraordinary hold over the people. Their services are actively, even if secretly, sought out by believers, often including Christian leaders. It is imperative that the community consider these healers as part of the team and bring their power to the service of people.

Finally, there is a strong cultural trait about the use of authority, at least among many tribes of Africa, which cannot be underestimated in this connection. In many tribes authority is held in common and exercised by the community. The elders as a whole hold authority and exercise it in the clan and the tribe. Effective team ministry would clearly mirror this cultural trait and would speak loudly to people used to it. The exercise of power by an individual, independently of the natural leaders of the community, is not conceivable and does not have a chance of success. By constituting team ministry, the church would recognize the importance of this aspect of life of many groups in the world and become more credible in the eyes of the church's membership and of the people in general.

HOW TO SET UP TEAM MINISTRY

I have tried to offer a brief description and explanation of team ministry, to share some of the major reasons for its necessity, and the challenges which it brings to ministers who are involved in it. In this part of the chapter I would like to reflect on some steps needed to set it up.

Dispelling Illusions about Team Ministry

Some religious leaders think that it is sufficient to put ministers together to secure team ministry. "The reason we don't have team minstry," they say, "is that we do not have ministers to assign to the same place or to the same ministry. If we had them, team ministry would be a reality." It is evident that to set up team ministry one needs more than one person. Numbers have something to do with it. However, this theory is based on the premise that the team is made up primarily of ordained ministers. And, of course, such ministers are few. But if we assume that teams can be made up of all sorts of people, then there would be plenty of personnel. Also, experience has taught us that when there was a number of ordained ministers together in big parishes or in religious communities or where this is still possible at present, nothing of what we see comes close to team ministry. Instead, we see frequent clashes and ministers going their own way. We notice destructive situations which bear no resemblance at all to team ministry. Just putting people together to exercise ministries in proximity to others can bring much trouble, little cooperation, and no great hope of real ministry to the people of God. Numbers alone do not constitute team ministry.

There are those who think that team ministry is possible if the participants in the experiment themselves choose to take part in it, making themselves available only as long as they wish. These people consider that it is sufficient for ministers to belong voluntarily to a team of ministers for team ministry to be established, and to function well. Certainly, a personal choice may contribute to the establishment of team ministry, and offer greater possibility of success. But this alone is no guarantee for a permanent establishment or for the smooth running of the team. Team ministry involves more than just an initial desire and willingness to belong to a team. Rather, it requires much more than just to exist and to operate. It requires understanding, a desire to grow together, and a willingness to be criticized and to cooperate, just to mention a few characteristics. These inner qualities cannot be guaranteed by the simple desire to belong to a team.

Another illusion about team ministry is that if the members have a similar theological education and spiritual formation they can constitute such a team and make it a success. The reasoning underlying this idea is that team ministry is based on a commonly shared vision of the church, ministry, authority, and that people who possess such a vision are best equipped for it. In theory, this seems logical, as it does that there is advantage gained than when the team members are not of a totally different theological background. But team ministry requires more than these qualities to exist and operate.

In countries where the tribal system still exists, there is a further illusion. People tend to think that if the ministers belong to the same tribe, have a common cultural background, the same worldview, follow the same customs and traditions, and know their own people well, team ministry can be easily established and its success guaranteed. To have a common cultural background or to know the language and traditions of the flock *can* be of great help in ministry. But they are no guarantee of the possibility and success of team ministry, because team ministry, though it may benefit from all these, nevertheless requires much more for its establishment and running.

Finally, many bishops, superiors of religious congregations, heads of offices and of parish councils think that what will help most in the formation of team ministry is Christian charity. They claim that there will always be people with different backgrounds and various theological views, who will bring to the team diverse personalities, various ways of looking at reality and of relating with others. This will not constitute an impediment to team ministry. The real impediment, they say, is a lack of charity among the members. If there is no Christian charity to help the members to accept each other, to understand the weaknesses of the others, to turn a blind eye to their faults, in the hope that the others do the same for us, to forgive each other's idiosyncracies and shortcomings, team ministry is impossible.

There is no difficulty in admitting that Christian charity plays a great role in our life and in our working together. Its role cannot be minimized. But to admit this is not the same as saying that Christian charity is the cure for all the difficulties most ministers experience in working and ministering together as a team. Anyone who is acquainted with the personnel office of a diocese or a religious congregation is well aware of all the difficulties encountered in placing personnel and assigning personnel to work together. I do not think we can come to the conclusion that there is little or no Christian charity among the priests or ministers in general. What we can conclude is that Christian charity alone will not guarantee the establishment, continuation, and success of team ministry. There are many other variables necessary for the setting up and running of such teams. If they are not there, not even Christian charity can make up for their lack.

Questioning the Basic Assumptions of the Members

The first assumption needing challenge is the expectation that all members of the team think the same way. Each member of a team comes with a set of assumptions. Since these assumptions are ingrained in each of them, and are part of them, they are taken for granted, and each member unconsciously thinks that all the other members operate on the same assumptions. Hence the members of the team are inclined to feel that pluralism is not a problem, since each one tends to believe that all the others think in the same way he or she does. And yet pluralism is inevitable when there are several people together. Their characters are different. Their theological education, their methodological approach to problems, their experiences, and many other aspects of human existence and interrelatedness may be different, and they too contribute to pluralism in a team. Members of the team must confront their responses to this inevitable situation and judge if they can live with it, use it as a means of growth, or whether it is a stumbling block to their membership in a team.

Another assumption to be questioned is the concept and use of authority. Some team members may think that only one person has the right to speak the last word. For them, all the other team members are consultative to that person who, if all other arguments fail, may exercise the power of veto to stop deliberations or to change them. Other team members may have an opposite understanding of authority and the way to exercise it. If these assumptions are not brought to light, they will create unpleasant and angry reactions on both sides.

A third assumption to be looked into is the basic understanding of ministry. Some members of the team may support the theory that only ordained men are full ministers and all the others are helpers. Others may think that all are ministers because of their baptism and confirmation. Some may want to stress the idea that all team members participate as priestly people, while others may wish to emphasize the notion of a substantial difference between the ordained and the nonordained. At any rate, this assumption needs to be discussed, because it will gravely affect the expectations of how things should be done by the team, the mutual relationship of the members, and the respect which each member owes to the others.

A fourth assumption which needs clarification is the male-female relationship in the team. Some may hold the view that men are more rational than women and women more sensitive than men. Others may think that men must hold the key positions in a team and leave to the women the ministries to the children and the old. Others may perceive women as men's helpers in ministry, as a kind of support system for what men are doing in ministry. There may be members who believe that women should not be team members at all or that they should not be ministering at or around the altar, but should remain in a kind of invisible anonymity. This assumption has to be questioned everywhere, but more so in third-world countries where the role of women is still in a kind of limbo, despite the fact that women everywhere are the backbone of most activities.

Probably the most urgent assumption to question is the understanding of the church and its role in the world. Some team members may perceive the church as exclusively, or primarily, a spiritual community, interested in and working for spiritual values only, with no involvement in the secular areas of the world. Some may understand the church as a visible institution with rules and regulations to follow, an authority to obey, traditions to defend, customs to perpetuate, and not open to any change, or perhaps only to peripheral ones. Some may perceive the church as co-extensive with the kingdom, or better the church *as* the kingdom. Then everything outside the church is not kingdom, is not God's, is not saved. Others may have the opposite conception of what the church is. Since team ministry reflects the views held on the church by all its members, and it operates in and through the church, it is imperative that this assumption be reviewed very early, and the position of each member stated clearly. The consequence of such sharing is too far-reaching for team ministry not to be pondered thoughtfully, and dealt with in honesty and complete openness.

I conclude this section noting that the purpose of discussing assumptions is not so much to determine which are the *true* ones. The purpose, instead, is to bring assumptions to the surface so that all the members of the team will become aware of them and understand why the various team members think and operate as they do.

At the end of the process, team members should know each other's assumptions and one of three things could happen. First, they may discover an affinity between their assumptions and be able to write a vision or mission statement for their team ministry. The team may, on the other hand, realize that there is a tremendous disparity of assumptions and decide that they need theological input to see whether the gap between their assumptions can be closed and common ground can be found to allow them to operate together. The team, finally, may conclude that, given the disparity of assumptions in its members, there is no possibility of working together and that it is better to dissolve the team.

Administering a Personality Test

There is another factor which enters into our behavior and even influences the formation of assumptions—temperament and personality. While the sharing of assumptions is a must for any team, the personality test is especially necessary for a team whose members not only plan together and meet periodically but work and live together. Personality tests can help a great deal towards revealing one's character and its influences on one's difficulties in interpersonal relationships and teamwork.

One of the most commonly used tests is the *Meyers-Briggs Type Indicator (Form G)*. This test is widely used and its validity is fairly high. If this test is considered too long, or a little too difficult, especially for people who are not used to undergoing such tests, I recommend a shorter version of it, the *Keirsey Temperament Sorter*. Besides being shorter, this second test is also easier. The questions allow for two answers only, are very short, very direct, and not too cumbersome. A few questions, which are worded in distinct North American slang, could be reviewed and rewritten to make them more understandable to non-Americans, or they could be explained by the person administering the test. The Keirsey test is part of a book, entitled *Please Understand Me: Character and Temperament Types*. The book offers a lot of information on how to read the findings of the test, how to interpret them, and how to apply them to the various temperaments.

Through these, or other similar tests, members of the team will become aware not only of their basic temperament but also of many aspects of their personality and behavior that are of importance to the team. They will become aware of their strengths and weaknesses; they will learn their communication style, both in content and process. They will be shown how they can approach and deal with people of the opposite or different temperament. They will be told of ways and means to recreate and relax. They will discover their natural qualities and possible problems if they are entrusted with a leadership role in the community. And finally, they will learn how well they can teach others, share with others, and help others through the use of their natural skills.

Providing Temporary Supervision

Once the team members have come to know each other through clarifying their assumptions and sharing information on each other's personality traits, styles of leadership, and communication, they are ready to commit themselves to the life and internal activities of the team—meetings, planning, evaluation, and team growth. At this time, they need to make a firm commitment to the team, whose assumptions and style of leadership and ministry have been defined. They need to depend on their faith, love, and Christian charity and all the other virtues to help them to be faithful and to cooperate. They will not be left on their own. They must know that they need help and will receive it as they move from knowledge of each other into action with each other.

The best person to provide this assistance is the one who helped the team members share their assumptions and who administered the personality test. This person knows the members of the team and can truly help them to get over the hurdles of their long journey. There is a need for supervising team members. This supervision could last from a few to several months, depending on the success of the team in coming together.

INTERNAL GROWTH OF TEAM MINISTRY

Earlier in this chapter, I attempted to describe the spirit and the style of work of team ministry. The description provided above is probably the optimum one could expect of the members of team ministry. They should strive always to fulfil it to the best of their ability. But they should also be reminded that it remains an ideal one approaches but seldom fully attains. It is important that the ideal be always before team members, but it is even more necessary that they work towards a gradual development of that ideal.

Praying Together

By praying together I do not mean that the team members say an introductory prayer before the meeting and a prayer at the closing. That is a formal prayer which often serves only to fulfil a custom common to the church gatherings. By praying together I mean establishing a relationship with God as a team, to help the members perceive God in and through the team and ministries. This prayerful relationship has to be supported through evenings of recollection, retreats, frequent celebrations of the eucharist, services of forgiveness and healing when necessary, and appropriate kinds of prayer in times of special need and conflict.

Prayerful Reflection

Prayer should permeate the reflections of the team in their deliberations and, in turn, the reflections should lead to prayer whenever the members feel the need for it. Team ministry implies working with and for the other members of the community, and making decisions which will affect the community. These decisions and deliberations cannot be achieved either only by voting or by forming coalitions within the team. They need serious reflection. The members of the team need to discover the will of God with and for the community they serve, and the call of God at any given time in its growth and in its life. They need to perceive the new direction inspired by the movement of the Spirit, which encourages change in order to follow the inspirations of the Spirit. They have to discern together the next step in the salvation history of their community, not in isolation, but in union with the rest of the world. Team ministry discerns the signs of God's times for a community in the context of the world's community. All this requires prayerful reflection, listening, and discernment.

Theological Awareness

Team ministry helps the community it serves to grow and to make decisions with and for the community. And so it needs to be informed of the new trends in disciplines impinging upon all areas of the community's life — for example, liturgy, sacraments, education, sociology, formation, economics, and psychology. God's manifestations in history are innumerable and ever-changing. The goal of God's interventions in history remain the same, but their external manifestations are modified according to the historical situation of the people. A theology which reflects upon these historical manifestations of God in the world cannot be stagnant. A liturgy which celebrates the personal and inculturated mysteries of Christ's life, death, and rising from the dead cannot remain static. Christian living, which is a response to the call of God within, cannot remain constant. Those who have reflected on God's revelation in past history cannot be satisfied with what they have already learned. They must be renewed, rather, in awareness that God is active also today.

Wounded Healers Needing Healing

In his book *The Wounded Healer,* Henri Nouwen captured one of the most fundamental realities appropriate to any team, but particularly to a team of ministers. The conviction that bishops, priests, and other ministers can stand tall above others, can weather the difficulties of life and of ministry unaided, that they do not need anybody to help them, is pure nonsense. And it may point to a deep insecurity and selfishness on the part of ministers.

That participants in team ministry are ministers to each other is fundamental to team ministry. Each of them has a particular charism from which the others can benefit, on which they can rely, and which they draw strength from. But team ministry also requires that its members find help, solace, comfort, and strength in the people they serve in the Christian community. The Spirit of God does not reserve gifts for those who are officially considered ministers in the community. The Spirit is completely free in the bestowal of gifts.

THE OPERATION OF TEAM MINISTRY

The interior life of team ministry is of paramount importance not only because it determines the quality of its existence, but also because it influences its external operations. Yet these external operations need to be based on and nurtured by other elements which may not be as important as the inner life of the team, but which bear on the credibility and the efficiency of the team.

Activities towards Radical Change

It is my conviction that team ministry has been inspired by the Spirit not only because it is in keeping with the style of ministry willed by Christ, but also because it promotes change in a more dynamic and communal way. I said above that our God is a God of newness, a God who promotes the growth of the people, a God who draws humanity towards becoming God's family and life towards becoming God's kingdom. Anyone who wants to follow that God cannot remain static, cannot live in the past or in the status quo, but must be continually enlightened and empowered by the Spirit, must move with the God of history, and must always be ready to accept new challenges and promote change.

If individual Christians have to be "as holy as the heavenly Father," if Christian communities have to mirror on earth the life of the Trinity, if the church has to be the sacrament of God's presence in the world, then there is no limit to growth, there is no end to our journey, and there is no limit to the horizons of Christian living.

Team ministry exists so that people can be better helped in their response to God. These people need help as individuals, as small communities, and as cells within the greater community of the church and of humanity. The changes called for by team ministry are not cosmetic. They are not a human palliative used to quiet conscience and to placate those for whom progress is never far-reaching enough. They are radical changes brought about by the Spirit of God, contained in the preaching of the Lord, and manifested in his life and examples.

Some of these changes affect the individual Christian. Christians are called to holiness, and yet many seem to be content with mediocrity. Christians are invited to accept the beatitudes as their magna charta, but many of them resort to substitutes which bear little resemblance to the beatitudes. Christians are challenged by the teaching of Jesus, but many of them find refuge in diluted human doctrines. Christians are called to be the light of the world, but a great many are afraid of the truth, of dialogue, or of any dissent. Christians are called to radical discipleship, but many seem satisfied with "following from afar."

Other changes affect the community of believers. Christians are summoned to community that they may scatter the seed of the Good News in the world. They are invited to experience the intimacy of community that they may bring love to the world. They are called to union among themselves that they may become communion in the world. Christian communities do not exist for themselves, but in order to extend the benefits experienced in those communities to other people. And yet, despite the fact that all programs which are meant to build our communities contain a strong appeal to action and to involvement outside the community, many prefer to shut themselves in an upper room, comfortable only in their sacristies.

Team ministry will be the catalyst of these changes, the promoter of them all, the supporter of the efforts of individuals and of community to implement them, the energizer for those who are weak, the stimulus for those who falter, the example for all to see and to follow. One of the major concerns of team ministry is to study change, to motivate for change, and to promote change.

Leadership in Team Ministry

Leadership in the context of change and teams is not understood primarily in juridical terms but in moral terms.

We can readily admit that in a team there needs to be a person who is juridically responsible for it. Above we discussed how that responsibility should be understood and exercised. But here a question arises: Should one person retain responsibility for the team for long periods of time? Or should the team use other systems — such as a rotation system of leadership? Experience shows that either system is possible and workable. The choice should be left to the team. In team ministry all members are equal, but each member has a different charism. It may be that one member has a special charism for leadership, which enables him or her to be a good listener. The team may choose this person as its de facto leader, even if he or she is not the juridical head. Or the team may choose to give all its members the chance to lead in turns. Each member has a slightly different way of exercising leadership and that may be considered enriching rather than confusing and threatening. This rotation would be one more way of stressing the precious gift which each member offers to the team, and how much treasured and valued by the others each member is.

Voting or Consensus?

Because team ministry is change-oriented, it has to make decisions which will affect the community it serves. How are those decisions to be arrived at? Should team ministry follow *Robert's Rules Of Order,* or some other rules which propose voting and majority decision as the only way of deciding the issues? Or should team ministry opt for consensus-building so that decisions arrived at will be adopted by all with no serious objections?

If the issues are about peripheral elements of the life of the community, then not much time should be spent on their solution. So the system based on a majority vote could help speed up the process. If the issues are about essential "gospel-related" elements of the life of the community then the members of the team may want to use a consensus-process of deliberation. In the consensus process, it is imperative that no member of the team have serious, substantial objections to what is proposed. For as long as such objections persist, the community will be disunited. The red signal stopping the process consists in the "serious," or "conscience" objections of even one member. But one must never expect the complete satisfaction of everyone in all aspects of all issues.

With the People

Ministries in the church ought not to be exercised exclusively or even primarily *for* the people but *with* the people. Team ministry acknowledges this reality and abides by it. To be *with the people* is to avoid living in the unreality of the ivory tower. To struggle with the people is to be realistic about life in all its vicissitudes and demands without losing enthusiasm for it. To walk with the people is to follow the prompting of the Spirit manifested in their lives. To minister with the people is to tap the richest resources of life, of inspiration, and, at the same time, to express respect for the people and their charisms. Separation from the people spells disaster for ministers, frustration for the people, and lost opportunities for both. Mutuality in ministry, not only among the members of the team, but also between the team and the people, is a way of enriching each other. It provides the opportunity for prophetic calls to each other. At times, ministers need to be called by the people to inculturated and historicized ministry. And at other times the people need to be called by the team to a more radical gospel way of life, to a deeper sense of justice, and to a wider horizon of vision and action.

What is important is that there be a constant flow from the people to the ministers and back again, that there be a complete opening of one to the other, and that there be a sincere attempt to be in touch with one another so that ministers and people become like two poles of an electric circuit. Light, warmth, and energy can be generated only when the two poles are connected. Without that connection, there is only stagnation, lifelessness, or one-way flow of activity without reciprocity. The ministers who are in constant contact with the people bring to the team concrete situations and real life in all aspects. They take to the people the reflections and recommendations, arrived at after prayerful reflection, for discussion and implementation. The burden of collecting experiences, of analyzing them, of achieving a consensus on and implementing the deliberations should be shouldered by both ministers and people. It is a joint effort from which no one is exempted, but in which all are part of the process of achieving consensus and of its implementation.

Acting Locally and Thinking Globally

Ministering even to a small community in a rural area but more so in urban areas requires that team ministry act locally and think globally. The world today has become a small village. People are linked together as never before by the mass media, by fast transportation, and by instant communication. Through the radio, even in the most remote places, people living at the most primitive stage of modern development are plunged into world realities. They become aware of what is going on all over the world and are spectators of world events. Through the mass media, all nations become our neighbors. At present, no real planning can be made and no effective local ministry can be performed without considering both the local and the global and the ramifications.

Team ministry has to minister to real people in a particular place but never in isolation from the rest of humankind. Ministering without taking local situations into account is to minister in an a-culturated way. Ministering without keeping in mind the global realities develops a tunnel vision with the risk of committing horrible injustices and depriving our congregations of the chance to become forerunners in the race towards a global humanity.

A Preferential Option for the Poor

One of the most striking realities of our global existence is that the greatest majority of our brothers and sisters live in situations which are not compatible with their human and spiritual dignity. The statistics are there to tell us of these realities: the direct experience of ministers who serve the poor and disadvantaged is also there to haunt us and to shatter us. The Christian churches at high levels, such as the Vatican and the World Council of Churches issue admirable statements about the poor and the need even to develop a preferential option for them. The rhetoric is good; but the actions often do not correspond to the words. In fact, as soon as some communities come to challenging conclusions about it, they are chastised, cautioned, warned, and even punished. As long as the church seeks to minister to the poor without disturbing the way of life, the politics, and the economics of well-to-do Christians, they are praised and considered models of true service to the poor. But as soon as they challenge the injustice of big donors and big corporations, they become suspect.

If team ministry wants to move towards change, it must face this challenge squarely and evangelically. The way to implement it has to be studied contextually, and actions must be planned according to the concrete situations of the people affected. But the obligation to implement radical change cannot be questioned, postponed indefinitely, or allowed to lapse entirely. One of the greatest scandals of our age is the way churches are still linked with the powerful, the rich, and the oppressors. How little of their energy is spent on defending the poor and on allowing their ministers to move with and to support the struggle of the poor.

CONCLUSION

Ministries are ways and means to fulfil the church's mission in the world. They should be based on scriptural insights, they should be exercised after the examples of Jesus, and they should respond to the various needs of the people in any given place, at any given time. Ministries have been understood and practiced in the church in many ways. At present, given the general historical situation of a world in which we are more aware of cultural differences and sharing responsibility is becoming more common, it seems that team ministry is probably the best way of exercising ministry. If this is so for the church generally, it is even more important for the churches of the Third World, where particular cultural and historical circumstances require such approaches with greater urgency. At present, the Spirit seems to inspire us with this model of ministry. The church and its hierarchical ministers cannot legitimately suppress the voice of the Spirit, or be deaf to its summons. To follow the lead of the Spirit is to follow the light of God in history. To disregard it is to walk in darkness.

Some people think that team ministry is but one more way of organizing the ministerial forces of the church. Others feel that team ministry is a substantially different way of understanding and practicing ministry in the church. Convinced of this latter perception, I have attempted to describe team ministry and to contrast it with other ways of ministry. I have endeavored to show the reasons for its importance, if not its necessity, for the whole church, but more so for the churches of the Third World. I have also attempted to offer some practical suggestions on how to go about setting up and operating it according to a gospel style of ministry. I have striven to dispel a few common illusions which accompany such attempts and to propose some ways of building up knowledge and cooperation among the members of the team and the people they serve. I have also suggested ways of keeping the team alive on the same gospel track with a local and global interest and vision. I can only hope and pray that the Spirit of the Lord will inspire many with this understanding and practice of ministry—an understanding and practice of ministry which would make ministry faithful to the Spirit's call, relevant to the historical circumstances of our times, and meaningful to the needs of the people.

6

A SPIRITUALITY FOR
CROSS-CULTURAL MINISTERS

In the last three decades we have seen three categories of missioners or cross-cultural ministers. Each of these categories has been, at least partially, the fruit of the environment in which these ministers have lived and operated.

The decade of the 1960s witnessed the independence of many third-world countries. This phenomenon gave rise to a great hope for a better future. The people liberated from the colonial yoke thought that a new dawn had risen for them, and they looked forward to a brighter future, a greater opportunity for all to live a decent life, and to enjoy a greater freedom and self-determination. Missioners responded to these expectations and longings with programs of development. They became so involved in these programs that some people identified their ministries with development.

The decade of the 1970s opened the eyes of many people to the oppression inflicted upon them by neocolonialism—that is, by the economic exploitation, by the political maneuvering of their own leaders, as well as or even more by the leaders of the superpowers, and by the cultural superiority expressed in many ways by the former colonizers and by the new colonizers. The missioners responded to these threats, or to the real situations of oppression by nurturing hopes of freedom, by conscientizing the oppressed as to the roots of their more subtle and more sophisticated enslavement (Segundo 1972).

The 1980s seems to be marked by the great desire of individuals, groups and nations to discover their own identity. The dreams of independence were over with, the experience of powerlessness was real, the difficulties of progress became evident, the struggle for growth became painful. People began to wonder whether it was worth hoping for greater things, useful to engage in the process of change, and whether there was in them that power to continue the peaceful fight for a brighter future. Individuals and groups

93

were confused, frustrated, and did not know what direction to follow, what to expect from life, from governments, or from themselves, from friends and friendly governments.

This search for identity has affected cross-cultural ministers of the church. Who are they? What are they supposed to do? Are they needed any longer? Is their time over, and is the only way to go, to go home? They are trying, almost frantically, to find a new terminology for themselves and their activities, new names to express their emerging or barely discovered roles and identity. This <u>search for identity</u> has brought the missioners in touch with their deep reality, and has given rise to a great desire for a deep and meaningful spirituality, and they have understood that "the call to mission derives, of its nature, from the call to holiness" (R.M. 90).

Cross-cultural ministers of the 1990s are in search of <u>deeper spirituality.</u> To satisfy this hunger and to complete this search, some of them are tossed from one current of spirituality to another, from one school of spirituality to another, and risk wasting time, energy, and efforts without satisfying their true desire for a meaningful missionary spirituality.

Hence some questions can be considered: Should missioners develop their own form of spirituality? How can it be developed? And if they should borrow elements developed by others who are not living their specific life, on what grounds should they do that? What would be the reasons for the choice? Would these elements be applied in exactly the same way, or would they be modified according to the distinctive situations of cross-cultural personnel?

My answer to these questions is that missioners ought to try to develop their own spirituality. And the point of departure ought to be the unique identity of the missioner.

IDENTITY OF A MISSIONER

It is not easy to describe theoretically the specific identity of the missionary vocation. Mission is not a static concept and reality. It is a dynamic reality. It varies from one situation to another, from one country to another. As the understanding and practices of mission change, so does the identity of the missioner. But given the present global trends, I feel that there are certain elements which could be considered common to all those who minister in a culture, in an environment, in situations which are different from the ones in which a person was born and grew up. These elements put together could give us at least a working definition of the identity of a cross-cultural minister, and in turn they could help us develop a spirituality for that type of minister. The elements which I will consider are a distilled version of the roles of the missioners described in chapter 1.

Missioners Are Persons of the Present

Missioners live in contact with present realities, with present-life situations. What is in front of them is important and not what is behind. What is present matters, and not what is past. The place where they are living, the people they share with and serve, the cultures of these people, their traditions, their symbols, their music, dances, way of relationship, and their epistemological and hermeneutical processes are relevant to missioners. The struggle of the people, their hopes and concerns, their vision of life, their experience of death, their cosmological theories, their methods of being community, their understanding of authority, their use of authority, their sexual drives, and their whole system of values are, or should be, of great importance to cross-cultural personnel. The religious beliefs of people, the prayers they say, the sacrifices they offer, the theology they have developed, the holy books they are nurtured by, are, or should be, of extreme relevance to missioners. Immersion in those realities to the point of absorbing them, and living according to them to the extent which is possible, characterizes a missioner.

Missioners Are Persons of the Beyond

Missioners have to go beyond themselves, their own personalities, in order to understand and empathize with other personalities living in completely different situations. They have to go beyond their own culture in order to experience other cultures, appreciate them, live in them, and act according to the specific elements of each culture. They have to go beyond their own history and merge in historical situations alien to them, which they had never lived in or even heard about before, to find in that history motives for pride, lessons for the future, bridges with the past, values for the present. Cross-cultural ministers have to go beyond their own values in order to discover values, to relearn what is acceptable, in good taste, and honorable, and to unlearn what before seemed to be the only way to be estimable and virtuous. They have to go beyond their own religion in order to appreciate other religions, to see in them unique means of communication of God with a people who have become God's people, and to perceive the beliefs of these people as salvific means for them and as expressions of their faith and love for God.

Missioners have to go beyond their mother tongue to learn other languages with totally different structures, vocabulary, and grammar. Missioners have to go beyond their native symbols which have helped them to express the innermost realities of their lives, to become acquainted with other symbols, whose value has to be learned, whose meaning has to be explained, and whose efficacy in relating to those inner realities is, for them, at best questionable. Missioners have to go beyond their own music, dances, and art expressions to become acquainted with, and eventually enjoy, music and musical instruments totally strange to their ears. Missioners have to go beyond their own church to discover church in every gathering of people who are intent in building the kingdom, in all communities that are dedicated to the progress of others, and in all groups that promote the welfare of people, out of religious, humanistic or social concern (A.G. 11, 23-24; Sobrino 1989, 40-42).

The now and the beyond of missioners are their most basic characteristics. Other characteristics can be found in the cross-cultural ministers, which relate to, or emanate from, the previous two. I will mention them very briefly.

Missioners Are Global Persons

Missioners are persons who cross over all sorts of boundaries: boundaries of culture, religion, language, values, logic, understanding, and awareness. But they do not burn the bridge behind. Indeed, at risk of mixing metaphors, one could say that they have to become bridges between cultures, religions, values, art. They have to help people of different backgrounds appreciate one another, accept one another, and live together. Cross-cultural personnel are individuals who live in and out of a culture, and move from one environment to another. They are persons with at least dual psychological citizenship, dual sets of values, dual understandings of reality, dual life, and, above all, dual culture. And they must be in love with both, appreciate both, adjust to them, assimilate them, feel comfortable in them, and become messengers of one to the other, and vice versa.

Missioners Are Persons Open to Surprises

For missioners the world is never the same. Cultures are not static, values fluctuate with the environment, absolutes are relativized, dogmatic awareness becomes redimensioned, the aseity of God is less perceivable than the historicity of God, the abstract tends to give way to the real, the fluid is more important than the static, and the beyond is more real than the present itself (Cobb 1975). God surprises cross-cultural ministers all the time. Their discoveries leave them in awe of a God who is constantly new, who continually renews all peoples with their cultures and ways of life. To become static is to miss the thrill of the new, of the changed, of growth. When missioners think that they have things rather clearly understood, well-thought out, well-defined, and well-put together, it is the moment of their biggest surprise. The biggest surprise of all is to realize that God is present wherever they go, that God has been at work there all the time, that "traces of the Word" are imprinted all over, and that the Spirit of God is very busy all over the world to bring life, and life in abundance to all, ready to pull down all those who oppose that action.

If we accept this as a tentative description of missionary uniqueness, how can we build a spirituality around it? Only those who have been in cross-cultural situations can do this. The scheme I will follow in attempting such a description is the traditional or classical one—describing the contemplative aspects of spirituality, and then the ascetical aspects.

CONTEMPLATION AND THE MISSIONER

Contemplation of God is certainly part of the Christian vocation for all disciples of the Lord. But it seems evident to me that the understanding and practice of contemplation varies according to individuals, their state of life, or their specific vocation. I cannot imagine that God would call married couples to the same contemplation as celibate persons, or missioners as monks or nuns. Each specific group in the church must be able to understand and live out contemplation in different ways, and yet attain the essence of contemplation—the direct or indirect sharing with God through the Lord in the Spirit (Gelpi 1978; Rahner 1985).

Definition and Types

Contemplation is a manifestation of God to humans. Our God is a personal God, who is capable of relating with others in an I-Thou relationship. And our God is also a loving person who desires to communicate with others, and ardently wishes to share with others. This contemplation can be direct or indirect. Direct contemplation consists in a communication of the absolute which is nonconcrete and beyond categories. God shares the self with others with no means. It is a person-to-person communication, heart-to-heart manifestation. Indirect contemplation is a communication of the absolute through intermediaries. God is perceived in concrete ways through creatures, images, events.

In both cases God is the major actor. God takes the initiative in the whole process, God chooses the ways to do it, the degree and the effects of it. Contemplation is an action of God who remains absolutely free throughout the whole process, and who alone determines all the modalities of that process. Humans can desire to receive the communication and can only be open to it, but they do not *cause* it. This point is of extreme importance for the proper understanding and practice of direct contemplation, but also of indirect contemplation.

Direct Contemplation

Direct contemplation is the immediate manifestation of God to humans. There are many ways which help humans to receive that sharing with God: yoga, transcendental meditation, Zen, centering prayer, the Jesus Prayer.

I prefer the centering prayer over the others and the reasons will be given later in the chapter.

If direct contemplation is a manifestation of God to us, then we ought to dispose ourselves to receive it. The means just mentioned perform that task. They help us to be available to God, so that God's manifestation can take place. Centering prayer offers very simple guidelines which are accessible to all in whatever situations they find themselves.

Whenever possible a person should choose a place which is quiet, where silence reigns. Apartness, being away from everything and everybody else, is an important aid to direct contemplation. This step offers us the chance to create a kind of vacuum which can be filled by God's presence and sharing (Pennington 1980, 67). But if this is not possible, then one should not panic—any place can be transformed into a sanctuary for communication with God.

A person should then adopt a posture which will help her or him to relax, to feel comfortable, so that the body is not an impediment to, but a supporter of, the exercise. One could sit in an armchair and stretch his or her legs on a stool, or one could sit on the floor and lean against the wall or against a support. The important thing here is that the position adopted is relaxing for the individual.

The next step is to close one's eyes so that one is totally concentrated on God and only on God, and leaves aside all creatures which could distract the person from attending to God who wishes to flood the person with the divine presence. One should not make these steps as a magical formula absolutely guaranteeing that contemplation will occur, but neither should they be underestimated.

A short prayer should be recited, in which one recognizes the presence of God at the center of one's being, acknowledges the desire of God to share, and the desire of the person to receive the sharing. One then asks God to keep all one's faculties centered on God alone through the power of the Spirit. This prayer serves as a reminder that God alone can make direct contemplation happen, that we are powerless, and that we depend totally on God and the Spirit for its occurrence.

One will then focus oneself at the center of self, not by thinking, visualizing, discoursing with God in the self, but by pulling all one's faculties inside and keeping them under control. In direct contemplation we are passive, we are receivers, we do not make it happen. Only God does. But we make ourselves available:

> To simply be to that wonderful Presence. It is simple, it is full, it is total . . . It is there we wish to stay, in a state of loving attention . . . To move in faith to God dwelling in our depth (Pennington 1980, 69-70).

To facilitate this being with, one can choose a mantra, a word which one can whisper to oneself when one's faculties wander away from God and

God alone. That word can be: Jesus, God, Lord, Spirit, Father. It acts as a breaker of the distractions which remove one's faculties from the center of the self where God is manifest to the person. We use it to help ourselves come back to the center where we wish to share with God.

God may choose to take over all our faculties, and to permeate them with the divine presence. If that happens, then one feels absorbed by someone else into a spaceless and timeless existence. One never completely loses the awareness of one's presence in a place, but one finds oneself in a kind of twilight situation where one is totally absorbed and yet never totally absent. If this happens, contemplation is a wonderful experience and religious practice is enhanced and facilitated by it.

Or God may choose to let one struggle between concentration and distractions, between presence and wandering away, between "being with" and "moving out of" the subject of contemplation. The mantra can help in this struggle, but not eliminate it.

If this happens, we should not panic or think that our prayer is not good or that we are wasting time. We should remember that contemplation is God's work, that God does not fail and so contemplation takes place all the time we make ourselves available to it, we dispose ourselves for it, and its fruits are equally good, no matter what our actual situation is. Remembering all this will help us to keep going and not to abandon the practice of contemplation.

The time for practicing contemplative prayer is up to the individual. Any time is good, as long as it helps the individual to concentrate and to be recollected. Sometimes the time goes so fast that one hardly realizes how much time has been engaged in contemplation. Sometimes it goes so slowly that one wishes it would be over quickly.

The frequency of contemplative prayer is also related to time. It seems that the minimum we can offer is a twenty-minute session a day. But as a person practices this type of prayer, especially when very busy, she or he may feel the need to contemplate for the same amount of time twice a day. The thirst and hunger for God increases to the degree of one's faithfulness to this type of prayer and of God's sharing with us. And the busier a person is, the greater the need is felt to use this centering prayer.

At the end of the prayer, one is advised to stop for a few moments, recite a prayer of thanksgiving to God, and to allow some transition between contemplation and action.

Why do I prefer this type of contemplative prayer to others for missioners? The reasons are very clear to me.

First of all this centering prayer is not so sophisticated as to become almost impossible for persons who are not professional contemplatives. It is among the simplest of all forms of prayer which attempt to help people contemplate God in themselves.

Secondly, centering prayer is based on a solid traditional Christian approach to contemplation. Its roots are deep and sink into the Eastern as well as the Western tradition of contemplation. The theological principles of contemplation, especially the indwelling of God in us, our incorporation in the Mystical Body of Christ, and the fact that we are temples of the Holy Spirit, are much more accentuated in centering prayer than in Christian adoptions of other forms of contemplative prayers, such as Zen, yoga, and Transcendental Meditation. The idea that contemplation is a gift of God to us, and God remains the only actor in the process, and we are the receivers, whose task is primarily to open up to God, is very dear to me as a missioner. We missioners are often tired and overburdened. Prayer often does not come easy. But this prayer does not require a lot of effort. It is an abandonment which soothes the body and the soul, while opening us to the infinite in us.

Thirdly, centering prayer presupposes human freedom. It does not impose anything. It suggests a certain procedure, it insists that certain things are very useful, but beyond that there is total freedom to operate as the Spirit inspires, and as the individual feels called, following the prompting of inner desires. This is good for ourselves as individuals, because we can apply even the simplest dynamics to our own character and personality, but it is extremely helpful to missioners, because they can practice it anywhere in the world, in contact with all sorts of people and traditions of meditation, even accepting some of the dynamics observed by other traditions.

Fourthly, the demand on our time by centering prayer is very reasonable. Missioners do not have much time at their disposal. They have to be available to others who come at any time, from far distant places, with urgent needs, and who deserve to be served. The volume and diversity of activities in most of the places where cross-cultural personnel operate seems to be increasing. Time is a rarity for missioners. This type of prayer does not call for much time, or long periods of absence from the tasks at hand. The short time we can set aside for it becomes a great source of strength, of comfort, and of intense spiritual riches.

Reasons for the Practice

Why should a missioner practice direct contemplation? The first reason lies in the importance of God in our lives. If God really means what we say it does—our all, our only desire, our purpose for living—then we need to be in direct contact with that God. For this to happen, we need to give time to God, and to God alone, to let that God flood our inner being and make it as much as possible like God's very being. We cannot claim that God is all for us, that we depend on God in everything, and then disregard that God, or just pay lip service to God. If the cry of the psalmist—"O God you are my God, for you I long, my soul is thirsting for you, my flesh is longing for you like a dry weary land without water" (Ps. 63)—is truly our cry, then we must open our soul to God and let God penetrate it with the benefits of water over parched land. Direct contemplation gives us the chance to open to God, and to be permeated by God to the very core of our being.

② Another reason is derived from the essential subject of our mission. If God is the ultimate subject of our mission, regardless of the model of mission we may embrace, then it stands to reason that we must know God in the best and most intimate way possible. If we really intend to deepen, through our mission and in contact with others, our relationship with God, and help others to do the same, we must know God well, not through bookish knowledge only, but through personal contact, through immediate participation in God's being, through the interpenetration of God in our soul and our life.

③ A third reason comes from the need that we have to become experts in indirect contemplation. To see God in and through others is facilitated by seeing God directly. But to perceive God in an indirect way will not be easy, or even possible, unless we are able to perceive God directly. Direct contemplation makes possible for us, or at least makes easier for us, the other type of contemplation, in which we ought to be experts.

④ The fourth reason is more of a psychological nature. Missioners live a hectic life; we are constantly under pressure; we face difficult situations which need a solution; and we are alone, or we do not have access to consultants and experts. How are we going to cope with all that, and not risk cracking up? How are we going to remain calm and yet enter into those situations with all our heart and mind? How are we going to grow in our faith and holiness, despite all that, or even because of that?

Cross-cultural ministers may have their own way to cope with what I have just described, and missionary congregations may have their own policies to help their members cope, such as shortening the time of service, lengthening the time of rest at home, giving more time for the annual vacation, and offering more frequent programs of ongoing formation. But my missionary experience and my contact with missioners all over the globe suggest that more missionaries benefit from the prayer of contemplation than from the other means mentioned above. This type of prayer truly soothes people, prepares them for the most difficult situations, and sustains them in the most exacting conditions of life. Realizing the presence of God in them revitalizes their strength, renews their energies, reconfirms their determination, and gives them peace of mind and soul and a sense of tranquillity which is difficult to describe.

Direct contemplation puts missioners in touch with the God who is the present, the real in their lives, and it reminds them of the God who comes transcendently into their lives. God as manifested to the missioner through contemplation is the same God perceived historically, existentially, and yet the ever-new and ever-changing God of the beyond. Contemplation enables missioners always to be in touch with what is in front of their eyes, to perceive it the way God perceives it, and it pushes them to transcendence that rests in the immanent presence of the divine.

To conclude, then, we can say that this type of contemplation is possible for missioners because it does not require extensive use of time and difficult dynamics. It is easy because it can be done anywhere and involves no strict rules imposed on those who practice it. But also it is necessary for missioners to use it, because it makes them much better ministers in cross-cultural situations, and it gives them the chance to perform in a much better and more Christian way in their ministries. And most of all this type of contemplation is in keeping with the identity of the cross-cultural minister. But missioners, despite their efforts and fidelity to this prayer, may sometimes remain amateurs, and may never become true experts in it. They are called to be true experts in indirect contemplation.

Indirect Contemplation

Indirect contemplation is the manifestation of God, of the Trinity, in and through creatures, events, concrete situations of our life. The God whose essence we receive through direct contemplation is also the God who lives in the universe, who continues the work of creation, of redemption and of the advancement of the kingdom on earth, and who communicates to us through the situations in which we live. It seems to me that this type of contemplation offers missioners the possibility of perceiving and sharing a historical God, a universal God, and yet a God who is always revealed anew. The Jesuit Rodrigo Mejia, writing about "seeking and finding God in all things" as the phrase which describes best the charism of St. Ignatius of Loyola, comments: "This contemplation is more than an exercise, it is a whole program of spiritual life" (Mejia 1986, 42).

Here I am not talking of means to be used, but of some of the channels in which we can perceive and receive God in and through others. These channels are primarily and directly related to cross-cultural personnel, so that they may see the importance of this type of contemplation and practice it.

God the creator communicates primarily through the universe, the cosmos. The wonders of creation are beyond any description, any imagination. Both the microcosm and the macrocosm can reveal the power, the magnificence, the beauty of this God. New inventions and discoveries made by modern technology have amplified this revelation of God to us in myriad ways. How much more right do we have to say with the psalmist:

Yahweh, our Lord, how great your name throughout the earth. Above the heavens is your majesty chanted . . . I look up at your heavens, made by your fingers, at the moon and stars you set in place—ah, what is man that you should spare a thought for him, the son of man that you should care for him? (Ps. 8)

Missioners very often live in places where the original beauty of the universe in all its flora and fauna is still visible, where the magnificence of the universe is not yet totally obscured by the pollution and the destruction perpetrated by the self-appointed lords of the earth. How can a person in Africa fail to be enchanted by the sky at night, by the enormous amount and variety of flowers and of animals of that land, and not be open to receive the creator God who communicates through those creatures?

But missioners have to go further. They must be able to discover the God who is universal, who operates and lives in all peoples, in all cultures, in all religions, in all events of people's lives. More than contemplating God in essence, they ought to contemplate God being manifested; more than contemplating God's inner life, they ought to contemplate God being revealed to them. And as missioners do contemplate in this way, through what they see, touch, are exposed to (the present), they ought to remember that these manifestations will continuously vary, not only from one person to another, one culture to another, one people to another, but within the same culture and people. The concreteness, historicity, universality, and "not-yetness" of these revelations are what should constitute the essence of the missioners' contemplation, the specific field of their contemplation. They ought to be proficient in it and to become the teachers of others. To be able to perceive the infinite God revealed in finite time and place, unfolding in history, living in peoples, and enshrined in cultures is one of the richest revelations of God, one of the most beautiful, one of the most enchanting, one which ought to attract missioners irresistibly, yet without artificiality and without losing touch with the world, its people, and the realities of the historical situation.

The Word of God will also be revealed to personnel in cross-cultural situations, more than to anybody else. These people, like anybody else, will perceive this Word in the Scriptures of the Jews and of the Christians, they will confess him in the person of Jesus, the incarnated Word. But they also have an ampler opportunity to marvel at that Word continuously uttered in the world, the incarnating Word, continuously expressed in cosmic events and in the multifaceted values of humans all over the globe. Missioners who are in contact with other world religions should be able to see prefigurations of the Word in them, as the early Christians were able to see them in the Judaic religion. They should be able to discover that Word wherever there are gospelled values, relationships, and fruits. They should perceive a revelation of that Word wherever they see a true religious leader who is able to awaken in the people a love for the kingdom or some of its aspects. Missioners should be able to see the incarnating Word in each community which shares, which relates to its members in justice, which prays together, which is gathered to deepen its sense of the divine and to promote the kingdom in the world.

But most of all, missioners ought to see the incarnating Word of God in the poor who struggle to eliminate poverty, in those who suffer for justice' sake, in the oppressed who claim their rights, in the powerless who ask for their rightful place in life, in the voiceless who try desperately to be heard, in the marginalized who refuse to accept their situation as final, in the exploited who cry out for equality, and in the downtrodden who seek to rise. The mystery of the Word is repeated in them—in their lives, deaths, and resurrections. They are the living and the incarnating, the suffering and the resurrecting Word, as Rahner professes, "Christ appears to us most surely in the poor and the suffering" (Rahner 1979b, 84).

This incarnate and incarnating Word should be the object of the missioner's contemplation. The Word who is, and yet is coming; the present Word and the not-yet Word.

Possibly the divine person closest to the missioner is the Spirit who reveals the present and prepares for the beyond. This Spirit manifests the unfathomable riches of God, the inexhaustible infinity of the Word in history and through cultures and within religions, because "the Spirit's presence and activity affect not only individuals, but also society and history, peoples, cultures and religions" (R.M. 28-29). Rahner proposes that we prepare ourselves to experience this Spirit in daily events. After listing many daily situations in which it could be experienced, he concludes:

> There we find what we Christians call the Holy Spirit of God ... There is the mysticism of everyday life, the discovery of God in all things; there is the sober intoxication of the Spirit, of which the Fathers and the liturgy speak which we cannot reject or despise, because it is real (Rahner 1979b, 22).

In this Spirit the beyond is normal, the unusual is regular, dreams become real, visions are concretized into reality, the impossible becomes possible, the unreachable becomes reachable. This Spirit is contemplated by the missioners as giving life to dry bones, offering hope even amid despair, opening avenues which were undreamed of, leading to paths that seemed inaccessible, and lifting people up to heights that appeared unattainable.

Missioners are daily witnesses of all these events, and should be able to contemplate in them the action of the Spirit. These same ministers, who are witnesses of the transcendent, will also find the Spirit to be the source of that beyond.

I feel that cross-cultural personnel can follow another model of indirect contemplation, one which is closer and more specific to them: *the way of doing justice*. According to Jeremiah "to do justice and righteousness, is to know God" (Jer. 22:13-17). And John claims that "anyone who loves is born of God and knows God" (John 4:7-8). Certainly the first step towards love is to practice justice. Christians of third-world countries, and especially those in Latin America, have well understood this point, and the missioners have learned it well from them. And they have coined a sentence which vividly expresses this reality: *Conoscer a Dios es obrar la justicia* (To know God is to do justice). And the verb "know" has to be understood in its biblical meaning, which includes the total communication of God to people. Missioners who have experienced this type of contemplation have become very fond of it. The God they felt was out of their reach because of all their multiple activities, and especially the ongoing struggle against the evil of injustice, has been revealed to them and to those who work for justice, to a degree never before imagined. The greatest contemplatives in our church are the people most involved in the battle for justice, for peace, for equality, for ecology, and for a new world order.

Through contemplation, these people have sharpened their perception of reality so much that they can see God present in all circumstances of life, but also they can sense the beyond, the new ways that God is moving into, and especially the absence of God in situations of evil which are made by humans and which are a constant denial of God and of the gospel.

The God who is present (reality), the God who is coming (beyond), and the God who is denied (absence), becomes very familiar to missioners who are attuned to that God in and through direct and indirect contemplation. Rahner summarizes all this beautifully when he says:

> Let us look for that experience in our own lives. Let us seek the specific experiences in which something like that happens to us. If we find them we have made the experience of the Spirit which we are talking about (Rahner 1985, 70).

Means of Indirect Contemplation

In order to be able to practice this type of contemplation, cross-cultural personnel should establish a simple structure which does not require moving away from or leaving places and people, searching out expensive retreats. This structure calls for the practice of "three Rs": Reality, Reflection, Response.

Reality is what conveys to missioners the presence, or absence, of God in human situations, events, and life. Immersion in these realities is a must for this type of contemplation. While the other type required apartness for its practice and its success, this requires total immersion in them. Not only immersion, but total presence of the missioner to them. The physical, intellectual, and emotional presence will enable the missioner to be a contemplative all day long. The people must feel that he or she is with them, is really present to them, is in contact with them, is listening to them, is one with them. The more the missioners are involved in the real situations of their people, the more they live with their people, the deeper the perception of the reality which surrounds them, and thus the greater the possibility of contemplation of that God who is and who acts in history through the events and people who become the signs of God's times. The world reality, the human reality, carries God within the present or reveals the absence of God. It discloses the present to missioners, and calls them to the future. Only with immersion, total presence, complete participation can they perceive God. A quote from Rodrigo Mejia (1986, 68-69) captures this dynamic very well:

> To find God in all things means then, to feel the divine will and experience permanent joy in accomplishing it in all the occupations of each day ... Mystical grace? Certainly. But is the whole spiritual life not a grace from God? The limits of asceticism and mysticism are difficult to establish ... But the gift of spiritual integration may be considered as a mystical gift even if, exteriorly, it does not make itself known in any extraordinary fashion. In fact, it is the mark of the mystical person to preserve this permanent devotion in all things, for there is a new outlook on the world, on history and on humankind, which causes one to exclaim like Jacob: "Yahweh is in this place and I never knew it!"

Reflection. The human reality disclosed by experience and critical reflection is fraught with difficulties (Meehan 1984, chap. 1). This reflection is not centered on abstract events, hypothetical ideas, ethereal dreams, or on the absoluteness of God. It must be concrete and it should lead missioners to a clear understanding of humanity in the light of the Scriptures, of human sciences, and of prayerful and communal discernment.

The Scriptures will play a great part in this reflection. They tell missioners how God acts in historical events and in human situations. They reveal the style of God's activity, the spirit of God's intervention, and the signs of God's presence or absence in those situations. The Scriptures are like a mirror for the missioners. In this mirror they can see reflected their own present situations and problems—not to find a solution for every problem, but to discover what God did in situations similar to their own.

Another means to be used, in order to become more sensitive to present realities and to discern in them the presence or absence of God is analysis based on the social sciences. The book by Peter Henriot and Joseph Holland on the topic, will be of tremendous help for the purposes of this chapter (1983).

This reflection on contemporary realities, with the assistance of the Scriptures and social analysis, should be conducted in a prayerful and communitarian way. Prayer in this sense is more than reciting formulas, reading poems, enjoying beautiful psalms. Prayer for the missioner is a shout of joy at the discovery of God in human history, a cry for help at the sight of godless situations in the world and in structures, a lament for the mistreatment of defenseless and powerless people. In a word, prayer for missioners is a natural reaction to all that is around them, a natural expression of their feelings about what God is doing here and now, about how people react and how the kingdom progresses or recedes.

This reflective prayer ought to be done in community with others who are committed to the gospel, to the same Kingdom. Such communitarian prayer helps to keep all those involved on the right path, to avoid illusions, personal deviations, misinterpretation, and deception caused by personal blindness, bias, and egoism.

Response is the third element of the contemplative structure for missioners. A response which is not manufactured elsewhere or mandated by others is the fruit of prayerful reflection. This response is incarnated in the realities in which people find themselves and it inserts the ministers and the community into all that God is doing there. It empowers the missioner also to counteract what is negative. This response is a yes to the present and to the beyond and it is a no to all that is contrary to God's manifestations and call.

Following this simple methodology, missioners who wish to practice indirect contemplation do not need to close their eyes. They do not need to withdraw from people to find God, but to live with them. One does not need to flee the marketplace to hear the whisper of God's Spirit, but to remain where it can be perceived as thunder. Consultation, meetings, direct contemplation will help indirect contemplation, but they will never replace the immersion in the social reality of local people. The experience of ongoing history is the essential means for indirect contemplation.

Reasons for the Practice of Indirect Contemplation

Missioners enjoy a unique opportunity to practice this kind of contemplation. They are often in contact with nature, and so they can still see the original beauty of nature. They are also in contact with different cultures, which enshrine God's work with a people and their response to God. And they are in contact with other religions, which enshrine the dialogue of God with people and the most intimate manifestations of God to people. They ought to become familiar with the God who is and lives in all creatures.

This type of contemplation will help cross-cultural ministers to keep working in the same direction as God. Direct contemplation fills them with God, and helps them become more like God. Indirect contemplation helps them to see God's manifestations in the here and now and keep their activities going in the same direction as the divine dynamic liberating people from evil. In the past, missioners committed serious mistakes, in their behavior, in their policies, and in their activities. How can one explain that people as dedicated as missioners, who were ready to sacrifice even their lives for the sake of the people they had been sent to, could be blind to the worth of cultures, to the importance of local and world religions, or could destroy in the name of God what God had already built in a culture? It is important not to be judgmental, but I suspect that such missioners never had, or had lost, the capability of perceiving God's presence. And as a consequence they were not able to insert themselves as agents of the love of God in the complexities of history. Instead, their dogmatic blinders kept them from appreciating God's multiple ways of being present. The tragic consequences of such inability are still evident in many countries. They haunt missioners like a bad memory. But who can tell us if we are not committing the same blunders at present? But certainly one of the means at our disposal to avoid such cramped visions of God's presence is indirect contemplation.

ASCETICAL ASPECTS OF MISSIONARY SPIRITUALITY

Contemplation is only one aspect of spirituality for cross-cultural personnel. Spirituality also requires the development of the theological virtues of the Christian life, as well as the moral and social virtues. Missioners should form these virtues according to their own identity.

Faith

Faith is of great importance in the lives of missioners. But not primarily a faith that helps them to understand theological formulas correctly, or to formulate precise theological expressions, or to develop abstract theories of God and God's interventions in the world. For missioners dogmatic certitudes are even hazier than for ministers who remain in their native culture. Rahner points this out clearly:

> Their [the faith statements] content is necessarily unclear for the very reason that they express man's absolute truth, as, of course, the original, undefinable mystery. This goes unnoticed by those who live in a spiritual sociological environment of a homogeneous kind, for through lack of comparison or challenge they cannot be aware of their own particular manner of stating things. But today's world is highly differentiated; accordingly, we find all theological statements "inexact," complicated by thousands of concepts, analogies, additional questions as to their more precise meaning, all of them floating about in the haze (Rahner 1980, 117-18).

Missioners need to develop a faith that sharpens their eyes to see God around them, that heightens their perception of the Spirit at work in present events, that sensitizes their intuition of the signs of the times, that empowers them to detect gospel values wherever they may be found and act as an alarm to alert them to situations which are antigospel. Faith, then, is related to God and God's actions, but in the here-and-now of all human situations (R.M. 89).

Hope

Hope helps missioners to see beyond the concreteness of each situation and not to be mesmerized by complexity, nor to be disconcerted at new calls from God, but to welcome new challenges. Missioners are faced with many psychological, physical, cultural, political, and economic difficulties in their respective situations. They are also frequently faced with abysmal poverty. They witness terrible injustices. They are in contact with violent death, destruction, and manifold evils. And yet they must never be discouraged but look to the future with hope, knowing that the mystery of the resurrection, which is the central and most vital mystery of Christianity, is operative. Beyond death there is life; beyond the tomb there is resurrection; beyond oppression there is freedom; beyond poverty and injustice there is the kingdom. The very death, oppression, poverty, and injustice that are being inflicted upon God's people are seeds of life, of resurrection, and of kingdom, as they were for Christ. It is in the struggle against those evils that life and resurrection are already taking place.

Love

This is probably the most practical virtue for cross-cultural personnel (R.M. 89). Not an abstract love that is the fruit of ivory tower theological theories, but a robust and strong love such as Paul describes in the First Letter to the Corinthians. Love is patient and kind; and with that love missioners can accept all the limitations of their personality, of their experiences and values. Love is not jealous; and missioners do not envy the goodness found in others, nor do they boast of the unique experience of God in Christ that they alone may have. Love is not arrogant and rude; and cross-cultural ministers no longer try to eliminate what God has wrought in other peoples, in their cultures, and in their religious experiences.

Love does not insist on its own way; and missioners no longer present a Christianity which is Western as something superior which cannot be transformed by the cultures of other peoples. Love is not irritable or resentful; and missioners do not resent other denominations, other world religions, other ideologies, but accept all that is gospelled in them, and cooperate with all of them. Love does not rejoice over wrong, but rejoices in the right; and missioners are happy when good is done, no matter who does it; when the kingdom is promoted, regardless of who promotes it; when gospel values are engendered even by forces which may declare themselves anti-Christian.

Penance (*Metanoia*)

This is another virtue which missioners must develop according to their own identity (R.M. 88): self-sacrifice for the sake of mission. Not a self-imposed sacrifice recommended by many writers of spirituality. These are artificial means which may help people who are in cloisters or who do not live in the market place of life where the means of self-sacrifice are plentiful, offered to them without any effort to find them. Missioners' self-denial consists in accepting the difficulties presented to them in adapting to different modes of life, to strange social customs, to exotic foods, to almost impossible languages, to long safaris on land or on rivers, to almost unbearable hardships offered by the mission area, by lack of many things, by the isolation of the place, by the overcrowding, by the lack of communication, or by too much communication, and especially by the demands of the people. What a variety of ways to accept self-sacrifice, to exercise penance, to practice the *metanoia* demanded by the gospel. Nothing can be more demanding than the demands of cross-cultural ministry, or undertaking the role of bridge-builders. This is indeed the *kenosis* for the missioner.

Probably the greatest sacrifice, requiring the most constant exercise of self-denial, is the call to remain open to the signs of the times, and to be serious about the option for the poor made by the idealistic documents of most missionary institutes. This leads to some consideration on how to live two important virtues for missioners, be they religious, diocesan priests spending time as cross-cultural missioners, or lay missioners: the virtues of obedience and poverty.

Obedience

This virtue is understood by people in the church in various ways. Some choose to obey the scriptures in which they seek answers for their present questions. Others prefer to obey superiors and submit themselves to authorities. Still others prefer to discover the will of God in and through the community of which they are part. Some resort to prayer and they struggle to find the will of God in the silence of their own little prayer corner. These methods of finding out the will of God are certainly commendable, but I do not think they are always practical for missioners, whose context will determine the way they will discover the will of God and obey it.

As people inserted in the realities of their time, cross-cultural personnel ought to discover the will of God within these realities. History carries the living God, the operating God, the God present in the life and activities of human beings, the God who walks with people, who struggles with them, who accompanies them on their journey and pilgrimage. It is in those present realities that the missioners must discover the will of God and obey it.

But missioners also work for a transcendent God. And they must try very hard to discover the will of this God in the signs of the times. Those incipient movements in humanity and in the church which appeal to people of good will reveal to missioners the will of God for the future, and invite God's people to respond to this will. The God who walks with people is also the God who precedes them in the development of a better life. This

God helps people to understand the new directions which must be taken by means of signs which, if heeded, will hasten the development of this new life—but if unrecognized or disobeyed, will delay or even stifle it.

It is evident that these cross-cultural missioners are not alone in the discovery and the following of God's will. They need the help of the Scriptures to reflect upon present realities and upon the signs pointing to a better future. They need community in order not to be lonely dreamers, or isolated visionaries. They need authority for support and for coordination as they strive to accomplish what they have envisioned and feel called to. But if they meet opposition from structures, individuals, or groups that seem narrow-minded or prejudiced, then they must have the courage to follow their vision, and to respond to the call of God with and for their own communities. And this may be one of the most painful sacrifices that missioners are asked to offer as part of the price they have to pay to promote change in the direction of God's will. Obedience to that will for the sake of the kingdom is what characterizes the best missioners' virtue of obedience. Cardinal Pironio reminded the religious of the world of this duty when he wrote:

> The situation of religious in Central America merits special attention. I think that a judgment passed on them from abroad would be superficial. In particular, it would be unjust to condemn attitudes that, however questionable or even wrong, are intended as a response of faith to Jesus Christ, to the Church, and to the concrete historical situation of the people. There is a great deal of evangelical sacrifice in all of this. And much prayer (Cabestrero 1982, 10).

Poverty

This is another virtue which makes tremendous demands on cross-cultural ministers, especially in recent times. These missioners, who in former times, could set up a little kingdom for themselves and their co-workers, are now challenged by people and by the stark realities of millions of the poor to reconsider their style of living. And while missioners could once look at poverty through Western eyes (asking for permission if you were a religious, or helping the poor out of charity if you were not), today many missioners have taken seriously the preferential option for the poor (R.M. 37) and are making efforts to live up to the ideal of living in solidarity with and at the same economic level as the poor.

This option requires that missioners rediscover gospel values through the eyes of the poor, that they become one with the poor in search for a more authentic Christian life, that they live as much as possible like the poor, experiencing the poverty and the humiliations of poverty, become powerless as the poor are, join with the poor in the struggle for justice. In a word, that they live like and with the poor. But this sense of poverty extends to other areas of cross-cultural ministers' lives. It asks them to divest themselves of their cultural layers in order to be ready to absorb other cultures. It requires missioners to question their own native values in the light of other values. It demands that they be open to other religions and to all their expressions, so that they can appreciate them and even utilize these insights to understand Christianity more fully. In a word, poverty demands that cross-cultural ministers be naked in the face of other cultures and religions, so that they may not act out of preconceived ideas, but out of knowledge and experience.

Poverty asks that missioners enter into the struggle of the poor they serve by questioning the policies of the countries they come from, by confronting the injustices which the poor suffer at the hands of Northern nations' policies or that result from the activities of the multinationals or a diabolic military machine. To question these policies is all part of the poverty which missioners must embrace.

In responding evangelically to such realities, missioners do not need to resort to artificial means to be obedient and poor. Rather, they are offered such means in the situations in which they live. Accepting these opportunities, they join in the action of God saving history—simply by assimilating with the people they work with and for.

THE EUCHARIST

I turn my attention now to the eucharist. I choose this sacrament because the eucharist has a privileged place in Christian spirituality, and it ought to have a prominent place in the life and ministry of missioners. But how do they understand the eucharist and live it? What particular aspects should they highlight, and what practical ways should they choose to live it as the sacrament of their oneness with their people?

The eucharist as a sacrament offers appearances of bread and wine—and a reality, Christ. The eucharist is a mystery and points to a greater mystery. It is a physical reality, and conveys a mystical one. It is and it becomes. Eucharist is what missioners ought to be—people rooted in the present realities and yet people of the future. Missioners find in the eucharist the most perfect ideals for their own life. The eucharist is a reality, but the eucharist points to a greater reality. And the eucharist becomes a new reality in each individual who receives it. So do missioners. They are part of a Western reality although they seek point to a much greater reality.

The eucharist also says something very special to missioners and their ministry. It says that one should not theologize too much over the eucharist, nor moralize extensively concerning it, nor squabble over terminology surrounding it. One *does* eucharist in one's life. Missioners do eucharist when they introduce non-Western cultures to the church. They do eucharist when they learn values in other religions and share them with their sending churches. They do eucharist when they sanctify traditions unknown to the rest of the church. They are eucharist when they become bridges between the Catholic Church and other Christian denominations, between Christians and members of other world religions, and between Christians and followers of other ideologies. Missioners do eucharist especially when they feed the poor, when they help the oppressed, when they claim human rights for the downtrodden, when they oppose all sorts of injustices, and when they put their life on the line for their people. Rahner (1985, 156) expresses this well when he says:

As the sacrament of the heart of Christ, the Eucharist is the source of our love for our brothers and sisters, but it is also the judge of this love. The meaning of 1 Corinthians 11:29 will always remain true: by sins against the love of neighbor, we eat and drink judgment for ourselves in the Lord's Supper. If there is and should be one Church in one body of the Lord, which is bound together with the bond of true love, then that must be especially true for those who approach the same altar.

Missioners should try to *be* eucharist more than *preach* it, to live eucharist more than theologize over it, and do eucharist with their lives in order to be worthy to offer eucharist with and to their people. Missioners should not so much preach the eucharist, as live it, be it, and do it with the people, so that their communities will truly be eucharistic communities and the celebration of the eucharist will not be a mockery or a denial of what the eucharist truly stands for, offers us, and symbolizes for us.

CONCLUSION

Spirituality, as Jon Sobrino (1989, 46-49) notes, is a tremendously appealing word in the church at present. This thirst for the transcendent, for a personal relationship with God, and for contemplation is a blessing from God. We should rejoice that so many people are striving to develop this relationship and to quench this thirst, and we should see in this the power of the Spirit at work.

Missioners are also affected by this movement. They too are looking for a deep, personal relationship with God and for ways of prayer and contemplation which can satisfy their hunger for God, while giving them a better chance to fulfil their cross-cultural vocation and ministry. They, too, can be subject to illusions, to misguided orientations, and to individualistic tendencies, which can kill that drive even before it asserts itself properly. There is a need to be watchful, to be enlightened, and to be open and honest in the process of developing a spirituality that is in keeping with missioners' identity and that can truly fulfil their desire for God and their need to be totally devoted to their mission.

In this chapter I have tried to share my own understanding and practice of spirituality. I feel this spirituality animates my vocation and, at the same time, offers me the best opportunity to be close to God, familiar with the Spirit, in tune with the Word, and in deep and warm communion with the Trinity and all of creation. I have tried to show how a spirituality for missioners should be based on their identity and consonant with it, not simply be added to it. This identity should color the contemplative aspect of spirituality, as well as the ascetical and all the other elements proper to a Christian spirituality, so that it will be a spirituality truly meaningful to them. I have endeavored to avoid falling into the trap of individualistic and narcissistic tendencies and to present a spirituality which is an immersion in reality and not a cop out.

My hope is that this will be another step in a process whereby we missioners will come to grips with our own identity, and commit ourselves to developing a spirituality, or spiritualities, which will truly be ours, and which will help us as we struggle to be faithful to our God who calls us to holiness and to a demanding mission which more and more needs to be based on God and directed towards our neighbor and all of creation.

7

FORMATION OF CROSS-CULTURAL PERSONNEL

Vatican II has brought mission back into the heart of the church in its Decree on the Missions, *Ad Gentes*. Mission is no longer either a privilege for some members of the church or the task of specific group. All church members and institutions are asked to renew themselves in the light of mission and to assume responsibility for mission within their own call. Cross-cultural mission is no exception—the whole church must be involved in it and all members of the church are asked to participate in it, either directly or indirectly (A.G. 35-41; R.M. 2, 3, 11, 27, 40, 62-72).

Vatican II has also called the church not to exercise a disembodied mission, but a culturally incarnated mission—one which respects, is imbued with, reflects, and promotes local cultures and values (G.S. 62; R.M. 25, 52, 53).

In view of these, and similar changes called for and promoted by Vatican II, what type of preparation do future missionaries need? How are the church and mission agencies to help cross-cultural personnel prepare themselves adequately for their mission? In this chapter, I shall share some reflections on this topic and suggest some proposals which constitute a platform of basic ideas, rather than a how-to-do-it manual for missionary formation. I shall reflect on ways and means to prepare personnel for cross-cultural mission in general, not for mission in any given country or continent (King 1990).

What is the best environment in which future missionaries can come to a clearer understanding of their call? What attitudes should accompany them? How best can they equip themselves with a sense of universality, adaptability, respect, acceptance, as well as a capacity to engage in a healthy and enlightened analysis and criticism of cultures?

The content of this chapter is directly pertinent to candidates who belong to male religious institutes or movements, and who wish to dedicate themselves to mission for life. But mutatis mutandis it can also be applied to other types of missionaries. The reflections which follow have been developed in the light of the megatrends and the consequent roles for cross-cultural personnel mentioned in chapter 1, and the following chapters on mission and ministries.

FORMATION TO INCULTURATION

The first megatrend which affects the church in its mission is *culturalism,* or the resurgence and revival of the importance of culture for each people. The response to be given by the church in its mission is *inculturation.* All cross-cultural ministers must be ready to face the phenomenon of inculturation everywhere and train themselves to perform a mission which is relevant to local cultures. To become missionaries sensitive to culture and open to inculturation, both candidates and formation personnel could consider the following steps.

Develop Some Basic Knowledge about Inculturation

A short synopsis of the major ideas about inculturation can be formulated as follows. Inculturation is not a moment, a temporary effort, or even a stage that, once achieved, remains the same forever. It is a goal which requires continuous efforts and is like a spiral which has a beginning but no end.

Inculturation is not the mere dream of zealous anthropologists, an effort by nostalgic people who want to preserve the past, or the plan of some theologians searching for exotic new ideas. When, in a 1982 address, Pope John Paul II defined culture as "that through which man becomes more man, is more, enters more into being . . . the foundation of man's ability to discover and utilize all his resources," he logically could draw upon principles he had enuniciated in an address to the bishops of Ghana in 1980, when he said that "[inculturation] is a work of God, it is an activity of the living Body of Christ, it is a requirement of the Church." Could we have stronger words than these to inculcate in future missionaries the idea that inculturation is a must for all of them and not just a choice based on personal preference? The pope also gives the major theological reason for this necessity when he states in speaking to the bishops of Kenya in 1980 that "inculturation is a reflection of the Incarnation of the Word."

Inculturation as Encounter and Merger

Inculturation consists in an encounter between the gospel, the church, and Christian life and a local culture, traditional systems of thought, values, and religiosity—which are already the fruit of human efforts under divine inspiration (Waliggo 1986, 22-23). In this encounter, similarities are perceived between many aspects of the gospel and a given culture, and they merge into each other. The gospel, with its values, penetrates into the culture, supports those values and elements which are in conformity with it, and challenges those which are contrary. And, for its part, according to John Paul II, a culture reacts to the gospel and "brings forth, from its own living traditions, original expressions of Christian life, celebration and thought . . . Thus, not only is Christ relevant to Africa, but Christ, in the members of his Body, is himself African." These words indicate clearly that in this encounter, new forms of theology (thought), of liturgy (celebration), and of moral behavior (Christian life) will emerge from the process.

The outcome of inculturation is the same as that of incarnation. Two realities meet together, penetrate each other, and unite to give rise to a new reality. These two components remain present, but each is enriched by the other, as well as each experiencing some *kenosis* from the other. Pluralism of theology, of liturgy and of Christian living is the most visible outcome of the process. The Christian theological principles are inserted into the philosophical or cosmic vision of each culture and a new theology is born. The liturgical principles are sifted through the existing rites and celebrations to give rise to a new liturgy. And fundamental elements of Christian praxis go through the customs and traditions of the people, and different ways of practicing Christianity are developed (Shorter 1988, 59-63; Schineller 1990, 68-70; Schreiter 1985, 18-19).

The primary agents of inculturation are the local people themselves — with their pastors, theologians, artists, musicians, poets, and writers. Above all, it is the lived experience of these people which becomes the humus in which the inculturation process takes root. The Pope expressed this very clearly when he stated to the bishops of Kenya: "I am close to you in every undertaking to make the gospel incarnate in the lives and cultures of your people."

All Christians and ministers who are not native to a culture are secondary agents in the process. All the others, even if they have lived in it for a long time and have an intellectual and personal knowledge of and appreciation for it, can never claim to be fully its sons and daughters.

This does not exclude a dynamic participation of expatriates in the process of inculturation. On the contrary, the process calls for their active assistance. The role of expatriates, though, is sudsidiary. They can offer professional assistance, be of moral support, and provide motivation to sustain that difficult process. Above all they can provide the link with other cultures and other churches in the world. Since we live in a global era, this link is of paramount importance. Inculturation does not mean to create cultural islands but to help create a beautiful mosaic where each culture is one of the pieces, blending together with the others to bring forth the image of the cosmic Christ. What expatriates feel must be said should be said softly, and with simplicity.

Being able to "listen with the mind" is vital and means acquiring a sufficient academic and psychological preparation to equip a future missionary to cope with culture in a constructive way. Candidates for and ministers in cross-cultural mission must become acquainted with culture and cultural dynamics. This general knowledge should precede any study of a specific culture, which can take place once the candidate or missionary is already in the field.

Culture is a vital expression of the beliefs, relationships, celebrations, and the life of peoples. Even in the so-called developing countries, cultures are not only lived, but are written about. Very often the writers are natives who have absorbed the cultures from birth and, through their studies, have become experts in culture and in the process of cultural change and growth. Nobody expects that missionaries know everything about culture. What can be expected is that they have a general knowledge of culture, its internal dynamics, its encounter with other cultures, and consequent changes. And all this ought to be part of the studies of a future missionary.

This is no longer an impossibility, and should be very easy, given the fact that there is so much literature on the subject (Luzbetak 1989). And yet how many candidates, or even seasoned missionaries, have done any serious study of the subject? Even at present, one can hear young missionaries complaining because their academic preparation lacked this aspect, or older missionaries who confess to having been able to acquire only a superficial knowledge of the people they work with because they lack the training to go deeper.

Martin Buber speaks of two ways of listening: genuine listening and pseudo-listening (Buber 1984, 61-67, 131-34). The first requires that hearers make efforts to hear what the others are really saying, without filtering the words and expressions through cultural filters. In the second way, what is heard is altered by hearers. Here we are not talking of language only. Words themselves often can be understood, but the listening can nonetheless be faulty.

Prejudices seem to be the most common obstacles to genuine listening in cross-cultural situations. Prejudice can twist the hearing of what is being said and make true listening impossible. The slogans we hear commonly in cross-cultural situations and many of the generalizations made by expatriates in those situations are projections of their subconscious and past education. They are signs of prejudices and can become barriers to true hearing.

A superiority or inferiority complex can lead to hearing with contempt and fear. People affected by either can misunderstand or misconstrue what is being said. How many young candidates or older missionaries are there who still feel that their culture is far superior to the one in which they live! Or natives who think, at least in their subconscious, that theirs is much inferior. Some expatriates think that their theology and their church of origin are much more credible than the one they have adopted. Such attitudes do not promote true listening and do not prepare anyone for inculturation.

The capability of discernment is the fruit of a deep knowledge of Christianity, of culture and its dynamics, as well as of true listening to others. It is not easy to divest the gospel and Christianity of their cultural and historical layers and to perceive "the naked gospel" as Vincent Donovan calls it (Donovan 1982, 22-24). It is equally difficult to discern the real cultural values hidden under the layers of the traditional and the stagnant. And yet inculturation requires discovering the genuine forms both of the gospel and of culture. To inculturate, from the side of the missioner, means to offer the gospel in its essential and transcultural dimensions. Hence the necessity for the future missionary to acquire the best possible awareness of both the gospel and the host culture. This discernment and stripping become impossible when we privilege Western Christianity and the prevailing Western version of Christian praxis at the center of our mission vision.

Such tendencies to ethnocentrism are very strong in each person, in each group, and in each local church, including those of the Third World. At the meeting, for example, of third-world theologians held in Dar es Salaam in 1976, African and Asian theologians rebelled against those of Latin America, because they felt oppressed by the insistence of the Latinos on one type of liberation theology. As a consequence, Africans called their own meeting, whose purpose it was to initiate the process for the formulation of an African liberation theology (Kofi Appiah-Kubi 1979, 189-95). For each Christian, for each religious group, and for each local church, the fundamental criterion is only the gospel, and, as much as possible, a transcultural gospel. From this point of view, everything else can be reduced to its essentials.

Dialogue is the best way to avoid absolutizing the relative, divinizing the historical, and establishing constructive listening. This dialogue should be introduced at all levels of teaching and religious formation, and the capacity for it should be required of all candidates. It should be practiced in schools, meetings, communitarian planning and evaluation, and especially in the process of personal formation. A candidate to missionary life who cannot engage in it should not find a place in the exercise of mission based on inculturation.

Inculturation is neither a mimicking of others, nor the acceptance of a premanufactured product. It is, instead, a vital process whose outcome is various expressions of the same basic gospel. Future missionaries ought to accept this pluralism in theory and in praxis and to consider themselves enriched by it. If they cannnot, they will not be effective representatives of the global church.

Formation towards "Listening with the Heart"

Formation to listening with the mind helps to establish the intellectual, academic basis for inculturation. But alone it is not sufficient. To prepare future missionaries to become effective agents in the process of inculturation, there is a need also to include the heart in that process. This can be fostered by taking the following steps.

Each culture has marvelous aspects: an integral vision of life and a worldview. Cultures include deep insights into the mystery of life, meaningful celebrations of the mysteries of this life, and of the life to come, impressive rites of passage from birth to death and the afterlife, and marvelous webs of relationships which make family and social life precious. Finally, artistic expressions reveal the soul of the people and their aspirations.

Candidates to missionary life must sharpen their eyes to see these wonderful elements and train their hearts to value them, to rejoice in them, and even fall in love with them. Without this affective participation in the culture of other people, no one can be happy, no one can establish a home away from home. One will always remain a stranger. How it hurts to hear missionaries who have just moved into a new culture already criticizing it, not for what they know of it, but for what they imagine in it. Even sadder is to hear missionaries who return to their home countries with very little good to say about the culture in which they lived for years.

Future missionaries must learn how to appreciate newness, how to be happy in it, how to discover its beauty, its novelty, and its diversity. In order to help them, the institutes they belong to should provide a cross-cultural experience of several months or allow them to do some of their studies in a different culture. If that is not possible, they should at least spend the first few months of their residence in a new culture in contact with the people under the guidance of a person who can help them discover, appreciate, and love it. Nobody should be sent to do mission in a different culture without having gone through one of these experiences.

Culture is the fruit of a people's efforts under the guidance of the Spirit. Behind a culture, there are persons. Inculturation requires that these persons become friends of the expatriates. The latter must love the people to whom they are sent, to the point that they are befriended and become their extended family. Once these persons are loved, their culture is treasured, the listening becomes easier, and appreciation comes more natural. In his commemoration of the evangelization of the Slavic peoples, *Slavorum Apostoli,* Pope John Paul II wrote the following about the two brothers Cyril and Methodius:

> They desired to become similar in every respect to those to whom they were bringing the gospel; they wished to become part of those peoples and to share their lot in everything. Their generous decision to identify themselves with those people's life and traditions . . . made them true models for all the missionaries.

The heart makes each element of the culture brighter, and helps each become alive in the experience of the expatriates, and treasured by them with the tones of friendship and love. And yet how many expatriates can say that they had "friends" among the people they lived with? Or how many can say that they were truly happy, that they felt comfortable in their homes, or that they spent time and celebrated holidays with them? Missionaries cannot prepare themselves for inculturation without developing a deep love and appreciation of the people among whom they are to live.

This love for the people can be developed only by living with people so that true friendship is developed. Out of real friendship there emerges understanding, appreciation, and also the right to challenge one's friends and their culture.

Each culture has aspects which produce negative reactions among newcomers. At times, these expressions can even come across to the foreigner as loathsome ways of greeting, of relating, of expressing humor, and of singing. The missionary must learn not to stop at these external expressions but to penetrate deeper into their real substance and meaning. The way of greeting may be disagreeable, but the sincerity of the greeting should be perceived. The way of celebrating may hurt the feelings, but the soul of the celebration has to be grasped by intuition. The food may not look appetizing but the love with which it was prepared has to be sensed. The efforts to penetrate through the superficial aspects of culture will help us to appreciate its adherents, even when their customs are difficult to like.

Culture is a great treasure of ideas, of human religiosity, of social behavior, and of artistic expressions. It can become an enrichment to outsiders only if they are disposed to receive it, if they are anxious to be imbued with it, and if they believe that people can contribute to the enrichment of others. An open heart can always receive something. A closed heart remains impenetrable even to the most beautiful and highest cultural expressions. To be able to receive is essential to mutual cultural enrichment and to the process of inculturation.

Formation towards "Listening with the Spirit"

Each culture is the fruit of human cooperation with the action of the Spirit of God. It is a sacred creation. No culture is superior to another. All cultures are beautiful in themselves, even though any given culture may contain certain elements that are more or less developed than in another. Hence the necessity of dialogue for mutual enrichment. But the fact that each culture is the fruit of the Spirit determines certain consequences for inculturation and cultural dialogue, which future missionaries ought to be aware of and pay attention to.

The Spirit leads the people in their cultural development. The Spirit remains the perennial motivating factor of the integral development of peoples. But the Spirit's ways are not the same for all. At present, among the Christians of the southern hemisphere, there is a remarkable stirring of rebellion against all that is perceived as imposition from abroad and a strong desire for cultural identity. Future missionaries need to prepare themselves to follow these leads of the Spirit, should desire to speed up this movement, and expect to follow different paths from the ones trodden in their homeland.

Otto Maduro proposes humility as a virtue to counteract attitudes that many Northerners experience in the South when he says:

> Mission: humility or humiliation? If there is a single characteristic of the new way of doing mission that is truly novel and liberating, it is the quality and attitude of humility . . . Humility is the realization that I am no better or worse than anyone else born of the same God . . . Humility is, likewise, an attitude that understands why the other has been subjected to a history and biography of humiliation. Humiliation is that which forces another person, materially or spiritually, to "eat the dust," to prostrate oneself on the ground before another person, to disown one's identity as a creature of God . . . Over against this form of mission, I choose to speak of mission as humility, as the preferential option of the powerful to relinquish power before the weak, to help the other person recover a sense of herself or himself as an equal person, born of the same God. On the other hand the humility of the powerful who strip themselves of that power, is as liberating for the powerful, as it is for the oppressed (Maduro 1987).

These are the fruit of a transcultural horizon and overcome limits to the free action of the Spirit. God's Spirit operates as it wishes, where and when it pleases. It is not constrained by laws, by conventional methods, or by human predictions. Actually, it often breaks down conventional barriers, traditions, and methods accepted by many as unchangeable and confirmed by the past. Future missionaries have to learn how to follow the Spirit, not to predetermine or condition it. They have to adjust their own categories, not to impose them on its plan. Restricted ideas and limited horizons tend to absolutize the past and people drown in those enclosed seas. The Spirit invites them to swim in the ocean of pluralism and diversity.

The ways of the Spirit are not always clear and their contours are never revealed. We know that the Spirit wants inculturation, but to what degree? What elements must, or can, be inculturated? The anxiety and uncertainty of the journey remains. We know where the journey ends, but we do not know all the intermediate stops. And so, to risk, to try, to attempt, and to experiment are an absolute necessity. Untrodden paths hide surprises. But the journey must not be stopped by them. We learn as we journey. The future missionary who is afraid of surprises, who looks upon present changes as a betrayal of the past and of religion, and who feels a great deal of anxiety in adaptation and renewal, or who prefers canonical and mandatory regulations to the free movement of the Spirit will either not be able to help the process of inculturation or will find it a traumatic experience, which he will tend to resist rather than help. Inculturation is a new process for all. It remains an unexplored path to most. Those involved need to be ready to risk and to have the courage to risk.

FORMATION TO INTERNATIONALITY

The second megatrend in human society and the church that we discussed is globalization. Culturalism, or the need to assert one's culture, is felt at the same time as tendencies to globalization. The full process towards inculturation and globalization requires that one be rooted in a culture in order to transcend it and to be identified with a culture in order to recognize oneself in the multiculturalism of humanity. Future missionaries have to be prepared to respect and accept cultures for the sake of inculturation, but also for the sake of globalization. The universal face of humanity is made up of all the cultures. And the universal face of the church is made up of all inculturated churches. Future missionaries have to be trained to this sense of universalism also, because it is part of their vocation. In fact, missionaries will always be signs of universality, even when they help the inculturation of the local churches. Formation for universality, then, is not only a means to enrich oneself, but a school for mission (R.M. 55-57).

Globalization can best be promoted through experience. Missionary groups should provide this to all their candidates. At some point in the formative process, these candidates should move and live in an international community, where there are members from various nationalities and cultural backgrounds. No other kind of formation community can prepare the future missionaries adequately for a mission which is respectful of cultures and promotes universalism. If young candidates to missionary life do not have a chance to live in an international community, they will have a hard time developing the sense of culture and of multiculturalism, necessary in mission. The beauty of culture and the differences between cultures can best be experienced in a non-threatening situation.

But in order to make this experience possible, communities made up of members from various cultures must become truly international. Internationality does not consist primarily in putting together people from different cultures, but in allowing these people to be themselves, to be free to share their cultural heritage, to help others understand their customs, and to make the varied cultures of community members the focal points of formation. There cannot be internationality if the dominant culture of the community is that of the place of origin of the institute. From food to greetings, liturgical celebrations, visits to families, decorations, values, recreation, studies, and prayer, all should be marked with the seal of multiculturalism.

Some missionary communities set aside special weeks to learn about, live according to, and celebrate the culture of a given continent—Latin

American week or African week, for example. Members of the community coming from those continents take the responsibility to help others understand their culture, sample their food, and play their games. The Zairian Mass, the Misa Campesina, the Indian Mass, the Native American Mass are celebrated. Members of the public who come from the same continent and live in the areas of the house of formation are called to join and help with the cultural experiences of their land. The important thing here is to have a genuine experience and each member of the community should be encouraged to go through it with full participation.

The communities we are talking about here are located in a certain continent or nation. This home group should constitute the dominant culture for the whole community. To achieve this, superiors should make sure that the majority of the members are citizens of that continent and that some of the continent's best members are kept there. This ensures that the cultural environment of the home group remains strong since initiative will end in failure if only a few locals remain there and if they can not project a healthy cultural environment, claiming it for themselves and for the others.

Such formation centers must be dynamic international communities, inserted in a specific culture. Candidates from various countries can be sent to these centers so that they inculturate themselves in the culture where the community exists, and also to bring a contribution from their own culture to the dominant culture. There are two moments here—one of insertion, and one of enrichment. Both are important, but the first one is the more essential in the whole process. This priority must be kept in mind by the formators, as well as by the members of the community, and must be respected in praxis.

Those candidates who move into a different culture must know that they are no longer leaders at the new place. Instead, they will strain to catch up in the prevalent culture of the international community, learning, absorbing, and trying to become as much as possible like those born and bred to it. Candidates who try to create cultural islands patterned after their community of origin, frustrate the process of their own inculturation, and lose a unique opportunity to prepare for their future role as secondary agents of inculturation in the church.

It is evident that each international community must always integrally reflect the gospel as well as the essential charism of the institute or group. Each culture and each community must subject itself to the values and essential elements of the gospel and of the charism. The gospel and charism of the institute, when stripped bare of the cultural layers extraneous to them, become for each culture a challenge and invitation to growth. Each international community must constantly keep these supracultural elements in front of its members when making any decision which would affect the culture.

Formation to Ecumenism and Interfaith Dialogue

Another megatrend affecting the life of the church and its mission, which we have discussed, is the ecumenical and interfaith movement. Future missionaries ought to work at preparing themselves to take part in this phenomenon, and to engage in it positively.

Missionaries will inevitably come into contact with other Christian denominations and other religions in the exercise of their ministries. In fact, Christianity is a minority in the world's population. And, though it is true that the majority of Christians live in the southern hemisphere, it is also true that the majority of the population of the world occurs in the same part of the globe. And so missionaries will always be surrounded by and work closely with other religious institutions. They must become acquainted with their life and ministries, able to share the riches of their respective religious heritage, capable of cooperation to relieve the many needs of their people, and to further God's kingdom. Two aspects must be stressed in formation in this regard—(1) knowledge of these religions and denominations, and (2) experience of their prayer and ministerial life.

Formation to Ministry and Team Ministry

Another trend affecting the church and its mission is the new wave of ministries called forth by the Spirit, and a renewed understanding and practice of ministry. Ministry everywhere, but more so in the churches of the southern hemisphere, must be understood as service and be practiced in a collaborative and holistic way. In fact, wherever missionaries go, they will find an established local church, and they will often be called to be helpers rather than leaders. This phenomenon alone requires a deeper understanding of ministry as service of the local church. Missionaries will also find in these churches a great variety of ministries inspired by the Spirit. And so, they must be ready to learn from them and to harmonize their own ministry with all the others.

Candidates to cross-cultural missionary life ought to be minister servants, and to do all things from the humblest (like serving at tables) to the noblest (like serving in church). Minister servants do not make exaggerated claims and are not motivated by power, prestige, fame, and promotion. They are happy, instead, to "seek the lowliest and most demanding places" (R.M. 66) and give up everything else in the process. This attitude of unselfish service, and this capability of cooperation, must be fostered by all available means and be constantly evaluated in the process of admission to profession or orders. I shudder when I see candidates going to parishes and taking charge of the activities they are assigned to when it means displacing others, especially lay ministers.

To be a servant is a matter of attitude, and these attitudes are difficult to structure. Thus the director of formation has to work closely with the candidates, look at the way they offer their help in community and in pastoral experiences, at the way they cooperate with others, at the readiness with which they accept any task, at the humility with which they work in subordinate positions, and at their readiness to be available at the price of sacrifice. These attitudes must be discussed during the whole course of their formation, and necessary improvements must be tangible for candidates to be allowed to continue the formative process.

Formation towards a Deep, Universal Spirituality

Hunger and thirst for God is another megatrend which directly affects those in mission. Early in this book, I tried to sketch out a spirituality for missionaries in keeping with the megatrends and the basic characteristics of the missionary identity. Here I would like to add something more directly related to spirituality.

Candidates to cross-cultural mission must be rooted in God and their whole life must be permeated by the divine. They must be ready to share their experience of God and of Christ and not just to talk about God, as if God were someone foreign or an object of knowledge more than of love or a subject for sermons. This type of spirituality—centered on God, following the example of Jesus, developed in the power of the Spirit—must have some special characteristics for the future missionary. It must not be a dichotomized spirituality, but a holistic one—a spirituality which is intrinsically connected with life, development, and liberation. It is not spirituality *or* development *and* liberation, but spirituality *and* development *and* liberation. It must be a spirituality which is able to absorb influences from other religions. It must be a spirituality with a well-developed component of direct contemplation, as well as indirect contemplation in and through creatures. A future missionary must have the wings of an eagle to soar high in the sky of the divinity, and the eyes of an eagle to spot the faintest reverberations of the divinity on all creatures on earth.

Here again, it is not easy to suggest ways and means to promote this type of spirituality. Some of the suggestions made above are valid here too. But most of all, the future missionary must spend time with God, must be heard frequently talking with passion about God, and must keep immersed in the realities surrounding him or her. No dichotomy, no first and second, no sugary attitudes. Rather, rootedness in God, love for God, nurturing relationship with God, in the cosmic Christ, animated by the Spirit, for the promotion of the kingdom. And, since for Christians, this God has a human face and an earthly name, intense love for Christ and eagerness to share experiences of God in Christ are also expected.

Formation of Males for Healthy Relationships with Women

A megatrend which more and more affects the church and its mission is the increasing interaction of men and women in mission. In what follows,

I speak as a male to other men. This *is* a limited perspective, I am aware. Still, given the charged atmosphere in which such discussions today take place, it at least has the benefit of clarity of perspective and conscious self-limitation.

Women are more involved in the public life and activities of the church than ever before. The church in the southern hemisphere is no exception. Here women have an even greater involvement and impact than men. Male, celibate missionaries need to face the fact that their closest collaborators will be women and prepare themselves for that close collaboration, so that it may yield the greatest fruits while they avoid the inevitable and specific difficulties involved in such cooperation. Women, as teachers and students, should be present in the institutions of learning attended by the candidates, so that the insights and input of the two sexes be available, their respective mentalities and ways of thinking become familiar, the projects of study be tackled from different perspectives, and the camaraderie established in scholastic and extracurricular activities may help the process of socialization, whereby there can be joy, happiness, and respect for each other and their commitments. Candidates should be encouraged to consult with women teachers, counselors, and professionals they are in touch with in their spiritual, psychological, and social needs or difficulties. Women should be invited to preach days of recollection or to team up with male ministers to preach retreats, offer workshops and seminars on women's issues and interpersonal relationships. The sisters, female relatives, and friends of the candidates and of the institute should be part of the celebrations and events of the formation community, not only as spectators, but as active participants in the planning, preparation, and celebrations of liturgy, religious and social events. These and similar activities would provide a well-rounded formation and prepare male and female cross-cultural ministers to work together with maturity, respect, efficiency and mutuality.

Formation towards Globality

This aspect of formation flows from, reinforces and complements the others on internationality, ecumenism and interfaith dialogue. It stems from the trend towards global existence for humanity and the church. But here I intend to go a step further. Cross-cultural ministers, according to Pope John Paul II, must be at home everywhere, not only in religious quarters but with all sorts of people, including the many humanistic movements of our times (R.M. 37). The promotion of the kingdom of God has many and varied agents. God uses all sorts of people to bring about the kingdom. Missionaries who are always suspicious of others, especially the nonreligious movements and who frown upon collaboration with them, who are anxious about becoming contaminated by their ideologies will find it very hard to fit in as members of our global village and will be poor co-workers with all those called by God to promote the kingdom in so many different but complementary ways.

Here again, formation has a part to play. During the formative journey, candidates must be helped to see the good in what others do, to admire the many efforts of a variety of movements, and to give such works the support of prayer and personal involvement. To rub shoulders with so-called "humanists" can only expand the horizon of the future missionaries, make them aware of what God is doing beyond formalized religion, help them see the wonders of God outside the walls of the churches, and above all encounter God's agents wherever goodness is promoted, life is respected, justice is fostered, ecology is treasured, and familyhood is lived.

Formation towards a Preferential Option for the Poor

Since identification with the poor is one of the clearest megatrends affecting the church's mission, I would be remiss if I did not offer a few reflections on this aspect of missionary formation. Missionary formation would certainly be a failure if it did not prepare future missionaries to be poor, to choose the poor as one of their first priorities, to live with the poor, and to struggle with them. This is not an easy lesson to learn, or an easy aspect to develop in missionary formation anywhere, but more so in the churches of the South where people tend to equate education with prosperity and a good life, and where missionaries often live like any other middle-class person and are perceived as such. The glitter of wealth seduces also candidates to missionary life, and they will find it difficult to accept the demands of poverty and a style of life in keeping with that poverty if it is not brought to their attention.

Instructors have a difficult task to perform in this area. Oftentimes the structures themselves are not conducive to a style of poverty. The rules of the institutes, for instance, require that all that is necessary to the candidates be provided. Examples of older confreres who have made a credible option for the poor are few and far between. Poverty, in addition, is not something that can be legislated, and the option for the poor is not something that can be imposed. They are a free choice for the individual under the inspiration of the Spirit. The individual has to feel this call, and respond to it with radicality and joy.

Formation directors must provide opportunities for candidates to visit the poor, to spend time with them, to be exposed to them and their lives, as well as to be invited to join in the struggles, concerns, and hopes of the poor. Students should be encouraged to visit people in the slums and to share with them all that they put up with—the lack of fulfillment of the most fundamental needs of life, the humiliations they undergo, and their whole life as it is lived every day. The final choice to embrace poverty depends on the candidates themselves. Some may choose to make the preferential option for the poor and to exercise it with the poor themselves.

Others may make the option, but they can exercise it in a more affluent area with richer people. The latter must be serious about their option and, though they are living with the rich, they must live moderately, do away with all that is not necessary, not accept gifts which are not needed, and above all they must be the voice of the poor among the rich. They must help the rich to understand their responsibility in the creation and perpetuation of poverty and they must organize the rich so that they too become involved with the poor and their struggle.

A candidate who cannot make this choice, who does not want to make this choice, who does not show a concern for the poor, or who is not dedicated to the struggle of the poor in whatever ministry he or she is involved, should be questioned by instructors on whether or not he or she is fit for missionary life.

8

MARY AS INSPIRATION
OF GLOBAL EVANGELIZATION

Mary has long been an inspiration of evangelization in the Catholic tradition. The purpose of this chapter is to look at the global mission of the church today in the light of Mary so that those involved in it may draw inspiration and consolation from her, as they struggle to be faithful to Jesus' mission and relevant in the continuation of that mission in their times.

Following an inductive methodology, I will look first at the situations in which missioners find themselves. I will then compare these situations with those of Mary's life and mission, to discover the similarities and to take inspiration from the style and method with which she exercised her mission. I believe we learn from her an approach which will make those involved in mission true apostles in faithfulness to the signs of the times and the spirit of the gospel.

A NEW ERA

In the past, the global mission of the church was marked by several factors, which were considered very important by the missionaries. Together, they constituted the missioners' consolation. *Numbers* was one of these factors. The more numerous the baptized, the deeper the joy. The bigger the buildings and the institutions, the greater the consolation. All that could be counted, that could be quantified, that could show quantitative progress, was a source of satisfaction.

Another such factor was *charity,* the assistance offered by missionaries to the indigent and the needy. The indigent who received help to survive, the sick treated in mission hospitals or dispensaries, the children receiving free education in mission schools, and the orphans saved from certain death, were an inexhaustible source of consolation. This consolation became almost ecstasy when these means of helping others could be used as the bait for "catching souls." It is true that the missionaries did cure bodies, did teach minds, and did help the indigent. But the hidden agenda in many such efforts was to save souls. These means of relief, help, and development were considered efficacious not for their intrinsic value but for their salvific effects.

A third factor of joy and pride for missionaries was success at replicating the church from which they came. This was visible in all the areas of Christian life. They built structures similar to those of the village or city of origin; they transplanted organizations such as Catholic Action and the Legion of Mary without change; they founded religious life congregations with the same rule, habit, and traditions as those of the mother house of the congregation. Liturgy and sacraments were celebrated with the same signs, symbols, and gestures as those of the sending church. To be able to see in Africa, Asia, Latin America a Christianity and a church nearly the same as those of the missionaries was not only a sign of faithfulness but also a consolation.

Such factors helped create a paternalistic dependence of the "children" of the church of the "founder." The missionary who looked at such a church believed that he had established a Christian community nourished by him with words and sacraments. One of his chief consolations was to function like a little savior among the saved.

Such consolations helped sustain missionaries in their inevitable difficulties, sufferings, and hardships with the people and civil authorities. But the thought-world that justified such consolations is today accepted by few. This is not the missionary vision articulated in Vatican II and post-Vatican II documents such as *Evangelii Nuntiandi* and *Redemptoris Missio*. The motivation for mission today is of a different nature. The cross-cultural minister is counseled to be and happy to be with her people, to work with them, to journey with them, and to share with them. Numbers are not as important as quality of life. The desire for inculturation, the attempts to implement it, and the success achieved, however limited, are the new goal, not the creation of a replica of the home church. Integral development, which does not exclude relief and charity, is the new way of helping, seen as valuable in its own right and not as a means to entice people to the church.

To live and to operate in the transition between two eras is not an easy task. The need to move away from one and to plunge into the other has serious implications and makes far-reaching demands. And yet the move must be made. Mary can be our guide in this attempt. She too lived between two eras. For her and her people, it was not easy to accept a quantum leap in their history. From a covenant, understood by most to be exclusivist, to one which includes everybody. From a nationalistic understanding of salvation, to a global one. From a legalistic view of religious relationship and practices, to one based on the Spirit and love. From a conception of the Messiah of one people to one for all people. From a Messiah glorious, triumphant, and victorious over his political enemies, to the suffering, poor

Messiah, who through his death became victorious over all evils. Mary and few others made this transition in the first company of Jesus' followers. But this was their salvation and their joy (Lk. 1:46-48). What they did is what should happen to all those who minister in the global mission of the church.

Not only is one era of mission over and a new one dawning, but also one era in the history of humankind is coming to an end and a new one is beginning. The era of political-economic-religious nationalism is ending, and that of globalization, universalism, equality and respect for each person, culture, and religion is beginning.

We are often told that ours is a time of peace, and that there is no "declared war." And yet never before have there been so many undeclared wars as there are at present. Many Latin American countries fight against internal dictatorship, corruption, injustice, and domination by the North. Many African countries are being destroyed by civil wars. Asia and the Middle East are torn apart by religious wars. In the former Soviet Union and South Europe, wars and threats of wars daily find their way into our newspapers.

The philosophy and praxis of capitalism have given rise to economic-political dependence, and have split the world into the few rich and the great majority of the poor. Meanwhile, the philosophy and practice of communism created political-economic dependence, and divided the world into those who hope in the perfect realization of the kingdom on earth and those who expect it primarily in the next life (S.R.S. 14-26).

It is within this climate of fragmentary peace, actual violence, and of socio-economic-political-religious upheavals that we exercise our mission. It is to these global-cosmic problems that our missionary activities ought to be directed. The historical moment in which we are living is a difficult one. But so was that of Mary. The similarities are many and profound.

The highly extolled *Pax Romana* was only a facade covering deep dissatisfaction used to suffocate ardent desires for freedom and hide continuous fights and rebellions. One has only to remember the ferment in Palestine, including movements for freedom from the slaves and the total dissatisfaction of the masses with the status quo. This Pax Romana was, in effect, the fruit of injustices and of oppressors without conscience who would present themselves to the masses as liberators and would align themselves with local political and religious leaders, to whom special privileges were promised to continue their role of oppression of the masses.

Is this not what is happening in our times? Is this not what the superpowers and the international or transnational corporations are doing at present? Are they not lording it over peoples and nations in all aspects of their life? Do they not connive with local leaders who sell themselves, their countries, and independence to the richest and most powerful contenders? The climate in which we live is very similar to that in which Mary lived, and our mission, like that of Mary, must be exercised in *this* context, and not in another.

There is an alternative to a modern version of the old Pax Romana, one whose advocates are becoming more numerous. It is radical, but not extremist—discipleship of Jesus. Here there are involved the gospel radicalism and the peaceful commitment to radical change. The gospel, with all its radical demands, becomes a charter for radical discipleship. A nonviolent commitment, based on and expressed in protests, boycotts, and civil disobedience, becomes the invincible instrument for total change.

Even in this area, the example of Mary will illumine and guide us. Her times were as dramatic as ours. Several violent solutions were proposed to the people—for example, those of the Zealots (violent revolution) and that of the Essenes (complete isolation from the world). And then there is the option of degrading and immoral compromise followed by the majority of the people. Even if Jesus appeared to vacillate for a while between the two extremes, after the crisis of Galilee he took his own way, which encompassed a peaceful reaction to the status quo, the most complete dedication to his people, but without use of any force, except that of reason, witness of intense but respectful dialogue, and finally death (Echegaray 1984, 61-67).

Mary became aware of her mission and that of her son from Simeon—a salvific mission realized through suffering and personal sacrifice (Lk. 2:34-35). At the very beginning, she suffered being persecuted and became a refugee (Mt. 2:13-15). She walked alongside her son in the fight for justice and love. Finally she consummated her mission on Calvary where she stood at the foot of the cross (Jn. 19:25) as a heroine who still believed in the final victory of peaceful revolution over evil and all its allies. Neither violent revolution to change the world nor flight from it are seen in her. Rather, she was present in the struggle as a mother with the faith of a pilgrim. She hoped for the final victory from Yahweh who dethrones the mighty. She expected the word of justice from the God who sends the rich away empty. She depended for the outcome of the world struggle on the final intervention of that God who casts down the mighty from their thrones (Lk. 1:6-55). Her action was one of presence, of accompaniment, and of support for the protest of her son and his peaceful but revolutionary action for change.

Yes, some of us have vacillated between the two extremes. Very few have embraced the violent revolutionary option. Very few the flight from conflict. Some have compromised with the forces of money, oppression, and power. Many, one must, however, say have seemed insensitive to the demands of radical discipleship and strong but peaceful action to destroy evil in our day and to promote the good willed by Christ (Cullmann 1970, 8).

The Forces of Mission

In order to face difficult situations such as ours, there is need to rely on extraordinary forces. Since we exclude violence and since we are aware that the normal forces such as common sense, conventional wisdom, and political maneuvering do not suffice, we must look for others which will help us in mission.

The Holy Spirit, according to Pope John Paul II, is the most significant and most pervasive force of mission (R.M. 21-30). The pope affirms unequivocally that "the Holy Spirit remains the transcendent and principal agent . . . is indeed the principal agent of the whole of the Church's mission" (R.M. 21). And it cannot be otherwise. Scripture tells us that at the most crucial moments of salvation history, God flooded the earth with the presence of the Spirit—from creation to the miraculous liberation in the Exodus, to the difficult times of the judges, the kings, and the prophets, to the coming of God's Word. If this is a decisive moment in salvation history, then the same phenomenon ought to take place. And it is taking place to the point that some call this the era of the Holy Spirit (E.N. 75).

The signs of God's times, discovered and discerned by the community, in the light of the Scriptures and with the help of other sciences, is another significant force in mission. In difficult moments, it is necessary to proceed in the light of the Spirit on the paths of the Spirit, which become visible to us only through a process of communal discernment. Normally, the voice of the Spirit is not a thunder or an impetuous wind which sweeps people away. Rather, it is a gentle breeze.

Once the Spirit has been poured out and the signs of God's times have been read by the disciples, the will must be engaged in the continuation of God's mission on earth. Mission is not a condition or a call that one accepts if it is to one's liking or if it serves one's purpose. Mission is life for a Christian, and in particular for a missionary (R.M. 40, 65-66). Only a resolute will, like that of the martyrs of South Africa, of Latin America, of the Philippines, and many other places where mission is lived in a context of total sacrifice and complete risk, will urge us into a mission in the crucial situations of history.

Even in this, Mary can be an example for us. She began her mission by being full of grace (Lk. 1:28). She was consecrated in that mission by the descent of the Holy Spirit in the annunciation (Lk. 1:35). Part of her mission was to retain the words she had heard, pondering on the happenings of which she was part in Bethlehem, Cana, and the temple, "treasuring everything and pondering on it constantly" (Lk. 2:19). The other part of her mission was to follow the signs of God's times, with an iron will, up to the point of being misunderstood by others, treated by her son with harsh words (Mt. 12:48-50; Mk. 3:31-35; Lk. 11:27-28). Finally she completed her mission by her presence at Jesus' crucifixion (Jn. 19:25-27). In all this, there was no dualism between her being and her activity. In fact, as soon as she was filled with the Holy Spirit, she went with haste to help Elizabeth (Lk. 2:39-40). She was with her son on the roads of Palestine, even if at times she did not quite understand him (Mt. 13:53-58; Mk. 6:1-6; Lk. 4:16-30). And following him, she served the needy (Jn. 2:1-11). Mary teaches us that

the forces of mission are the Spirit, a determined will, and a resolute following of Jesus. Here is an equilibrium between being and acting, contemplation and action, God and humanity.

Mission of the Poor

One of the concrete situations in which mission is exercised seems to
dominate all the others—*the mission of the poor* (Motte 1987, 57-63). In
the traditional style of mission, the poor were the objects of charity from
the rich. Then they became objects of development—planned, financed,
controlled, and carried out by the nonpoor. Later on, the poor became
agents of development, but second-class agents, acting under the control
of the rich. Most recently, though, the role of the poor substantially altered,
and mission can not remain the same. The poor have emerged as those
who possess little, who have little power in society, and yet, moved by their
faith and love, work to correct injustices, to create a new world, and to
envisage a different church.

The poor have entered our history. They have heard the gospel anew,
as it was proclaimed by Jesus. They have perceived gospel values as Jesus
lived them, and have entered the church's life as part of a holistic revolution. The poor no longer want to be considered objects of compassion and
charity. Instead, they claim justice. Above all, they rebel against being
treated as objects of development planned by others and they claim the
right of being subjects of their own development. They are grateful to those
who help them but are unwilling to take the back seat.

This is not an idealization of the poor as persons. In fact, Sobrino is
careful to note that they are as human, as frail, and as sinful as everyone
else (Sobrino 1989, 27-28, 75, 84). Rather, this new view of the poor is an
acknowledgment of their values, of the process by which they achieve liberation, and of their ideals, dreams, hopes, and constancy. The cutting edge
mission of the church has shifted from work done by well-off Northerners
to that done by the poor. The agents of this mission are increasingly coming
from the Third World (Degrise 1984, 71-92). Mission will inexorably be
more the mission of the poor and for the poor—a reality difficult for missionaries from the North to understand and accept.

Here again the example of Mary may help us. Mary's mission was that
of a person with no power in the eyes of the citizens of her country. She
came from Galilee, the area farthest from the religious center of Judaism,
and the one with most frequent contacts with suspicious foreigners, the
"nations" of the Bible. Their geographic position made Galileans unacceptable to the religious and political leaders of the day and to a Jerusalem
establishment that looked upon them as potential traitors and rebels.

Mary also was poor as a person. As stated in the gospel, she experienced
deprivation in Bethlehem and was one of the poor in the presentation of

Jesus in the temple (Lk. 2:24). Above all, Mary lived under the political yoke and domination of foreigners (Lk. 2:1-5).

It was in these conditions that Mary exercised her mission—a marvelous example for all who are in mission today. But how difficult it is to understand that poverty and to live it. We must *voluntarily* become poor in the sense explained above in order to understand it. In fact, in today's mission, expatriates ought to take the backseat and be led by the poor, relinquishing any sense of superiority and authoritarianism.

I wish to offer reflections on these dynamics now. They are based on love and inspired by God's love. This love alone is the source of Yahweh's activities—"His mercy is from age to age on those who fear him" (Lk. 1:50). This merciful love becomes a bulwark, a wall against which all efforts of the oppressors and of the unjust will be smashed (Pss. 71, 77, 78, 101). Echegaray (1984, 87) explains this point briefly but cogently:

> God is love to be communicated, a life to be shared, a freedom and joy that are meant to inspire freedom and joy in human beings. For this very reason, the coming of God is the coming of a judgment against everything that attacks these values.

In the recent past, missionaries have had the chance to witness this love and its dynamics in the world. Colonizing powers crashed against that bulwark. While the poor and the oppressed regained freedom, the powerful and oppressors experienced defeat. These same dynamic forces still influence the decolonized nations. In fact, after the political liberation from the colonizers, internal oppressors have arisen to control the same people who had just overcome external oppression. And these, too, have been crushed by these forces, and have experienced the same defeat.

The process I have just referred to has taken place not only in the political arena but also in the religious field. Those ecclesial structures which do not respect the rights of members or native religious aspirations, and which have proven unjust and oppressive, have been either demolished by the revolutionary dynamics of God's mission in the world or, I believe, with David Clark, will be demolished in the future (Clark 1989, 27-44). This is an inexorable law—the love of God is merciful, compassionate, and the bulwark of justice against which the oppressors are shattered. Was not Mary told this in the temple? "Behold, this child is appointed for the rise and fall of many in Israel, and for a sign to be opposed?" (Lk. 2:34). Is this not what Mary understood so clearly from reflecting on the history of her people? Are these not the revolutionary dynamics which Luke incorporates in Mary's song, a synthesis of the whole missionary process of Yahweh in the history of Israel and of humanity (Lk.2:50-53)?

Mary highlights the side that Yahweh and her son support. They are not neutral in these revolutions. No, they have taken an irrevocable and clear stance for the poor. On which side are we? That is the crucial question.

And the answer to it is not always consoling. In fact, even if our rhetoric, like that of so many people in the church, including some of its leaders, echoes the Magnificat, our praxis frequently contradicts that song.

Mission has always posed questions to its agents. In the past, the challenges were primarily of a physical nature, consisting in the acceptance of daunting privations by missionaries. Such difficulties, severe though they were, could be faced by people with strong bodies. Although mission today does not exclude these difficulties in certain areas of the globe, challenges are now more psychological than physical. They originate mainly in a socio-political climate that demands a different role of the missionary—being accepted not because of skin color, learning, or other external factors, but because of his or her capacities as a person and as a religious leader. Another source of difficulty for Northerners stems from dealing with a church whose members live at different socio-economic levels, and whose pastoral needs are very different from their own. There are also the demands stemming from the need to be cross-cultural. In addition, there is the exigency to inculturate the gospel message and the church, with all its structures and ministries, which must be done by local Christians while foreigners are on the sidelines.

The challenges in the socio-political-economic arenas are perplexing—the conflict for supremacy between the various groups and tribes; the economic exploitation of the transnationals; and the misery and squalor of the great majority of the people. All this should prompt a strong response of justice in the heart of missionaries.

Here, too, we can look at Mary to see that she was subjected to similar challenges in her mission in order to take courage and inspiration from her. It is clear from Scripture that she went through uncommon challenges. They arose in the historical situations in which she lived, the place of birth, her condition as one of the poor, the determination of the political and religious authorities to get rid of her son, the misunderstandings and misconceptions of her own people and relatives, her doubts and uncertainties regarding her son, and his activities. Finally, she suffered because of the lack of understanding of those who lived with him. But they never stopped her mission.

She answered with unshakable faith in the fidelity of God. This faith helped her to accept her mission and its consequences—contained in the prophecy "a sword will pierce your heart." They led her even to Calvary, which must have seemed to be the defeat of mission. Faith in God's fidelity, which was her support in the difficult journey of her mission, was also one of the themes of her Magnificat—"God has come to the help of Israel his servant, mindful of his mercy, according to the promise he made to our ancestors, of his mercy to Abraham and to his descendants forever" (Lk. 1:54-55). Her unshakable faith was the reason for asking and obtaining her son's first miracle, even though his "hour" had not yet come. Faith sustained her and helped her enkindle faith in the hearts of his followers.

For missionaries who work in the slums or favellas, Marian faith in the fidelity of God for his poor is a great solace. For missionaries who work for radical change in the structures of society and the church, Marian faith in the fidelity of God to the kingdom preserves them healthy in mind and body.

Mary's faith did not impede her from posing questions, asking for explanations, and inquiring about events. It did not free her from doubts about what was happening around her — "How can this come about?" (Lk. 1:34). "Why have you done this to us?" she inquired of her son in the temple (Lk. 2:48). Faith is always a gift of God, in its development and as a process advanced by study and prayer.

Faith and doubts inevitably lead the missionary to ask frequent questions and require missionaries to take permanent formation seriously. The situations of mission change rapidly. To become intellectually and spiritually fossilized means the end of creative missionary work. It means the perpetuation of the status quo and stagnation. And yet many missionaries take pride in claiming that they have not opened a book since ordination or final profession! Such attitudes make it difficult for their societies to offer updating or for their bishops to implement changes and pastoral plans.

The challenges of mission, if accepted in all their complexity and magnitude, include the cross. This cross can take the form of open persecution, moral or physical ostracism, expulsion, torture, and even martyrdom. To close our eyes to this reality is to deny the experience of Jesus, Mary, and of the church for the last two thousand years. It was this way for Jesus and also for Mary and Joseph in Bethlehem, in the presentation in the temple, where Mary heard of the sword which would pierce her heart, in the misunderstandings of Mary about her son's mission, and finally in his physical death on the cross.

MARY AND THE UNIVERSAL MISSION OF ALL CHRISTIANS

Not many years ago, the external mission of the church was carried out by missionary institutes under the jurisdiction of the Congregation for the Propagation of the Faith (now the Congregation for the Evangelization of Peoples). Local ordinaries, the dioceses, and the laity were absent from it. Since the Second Vatican Council, "there is a new awareness that missionary activity is a matter for all Christians, for all dioceses and parishes, Church institutions and associations" (R.M. 2). It is no longer missionary orders working under Roman directives who are responsible for the mission. Bishops have taken a clear stance in the service of this mission as full partners, co-responsible for missionary activities. They offer personnel and support for world mission by entering into direct contact with other local churches and their pastors, establishing cooperation through bilateral agreements (R.M. 61-76). Thus missionary institutes are no longer the exclusive agents of mission—which now include *Fidei Donum* priests (diocesan priests on loan), religious, and laity who offer their help either for a specified period or for life.

A newer development has given a completely different twist to the universal mission of the church—the entrance and participation in the missionary apostolate by younger churches. Their presence is evidenced by the several missionary institutes recently established by younger churches and the service of thousands of third-world members in missionary and religious institutes founded in older churches—for example, in groups such as the Franciscans or Jesuits.

Here the example of Mary encourages the church in mission. She was a woman and a lay member of the earliest community. She was the disciple who lived for years with her son, the missionary of God to humanity. She prepared Jesus for the mission entrusted to him by the Father. At Cana she prodded him to begin his missionary life. Without belonging officially to the group of the apostles or of the seventy, she nevertheless followed him. With a few women and one apostle, she was present at his sufferings. With the newborn community of the believers, she awaited the coming of the Spirit that marked the beginning of the church's mission.

Is this not what has happened in the newly established churches? In Africa, a central place in the development of missionary work and in the expansion of the church, lay catechists and lay teachers were central in the spread of faith. They are the fathers and the mothers of the African churches, as several bishops stated at the 1987 synod on the laity. Lay people were responsible for the founding of the church in Korea and for its running for many years. Lay people constituted the bulk of ministers in Indonesia as well. The recent spiritual renewal of the Latin American churches is due to a great extent to the laity in the base Christian communities. The vitality of efforts to rekindle faith in the older churches of Europe and North America can often be traced to groups of laity—charismatics, Cursillo, marriage encounter, renewal, catechumenates, and a host of traditional activities run by lay people.

In our days, the Spirit is calling all to mission but in a particular way the laity. How are they received by the professional missionaries? Some missionaries are enthusiastic about the participation of the laity in mission and see in this phenomenon one of the greatest hopes for mission. Others behave as if mission were still primarily the task of the priests and religious. The majority try to make the laity into scaled-down versions of religious priests. Clericalism, which was recognized by many third-world bishops as the number one obstacle for the mission of the laity in the world and in the church, is still very strong with most missionaries. It endangers the participation of the laity in mission.

Among the laity, women are at the very bottom of the ladder. They are doubly penalized in the life and mission of the church. As the synod on the laity has pointed out clearly, they not only face the same difficulties as all other lay people, but others reserved for women only, such as the refusal of rights to serve at the altar and to participate fully in other official public ministries of the church. Thus, women remain the most marginalized of all the members of the church.

And yet, Mary was never a member of the clergy. She remained a lay person and exercised a unique mission—according to tradition, a role superior to that of any other member of the church. She did so as a woman and a lay person. Mary and other women had an extraordinary place in the mission of Jesus and at his death. They were there at the beginning of evangelization after the resurrection of Jesus, in the mission of the primitive church, and in the life and activities of the first communities and the house churches (Brown 1975, 92-96).

To take inspiration from Mary in this aspect of mission means to change completely the relationships of the male missionary with the laity in general and with women in particular—be they religious or lay—and to change the style of cooperation between clergy and laity in mission. It means to abandon the spirit of superiority and arrogance of clericalism, and to accept a method of ministry which respects the charisms of all and uses them in the most constructive and egalitarian way for the good of mission. It means to set up more humane and cordial methods of cooperation between all the forces in mission—step which would create an enterprise similar to that of Jesus who "came not to be served, but to serve, and to give his life for others."

MARY AND THE CORE OF MISSION

I will end this chapter by going more deeply into the content of mission. I am aware of the difficulty involved in treating this point, because it is part of the mystery of God. Nevertheless, I think that it is imperative that we ask this question: What is the core of mission, even if, for historical reasons, one or another aspect of that content has to be focused on to the seeming exclusion of others at any given moment? Finally how can Mary be our guide in this exploration?

Some hold that the *kingdom of God* ought to be the focal point of mission. In *Redemptoris Missio,* Pope John Paul II suggests that this aspect is essential to mission, if it is not mission itself (R.M. 12-20). To build the kingdom of God on earth is to continue the mission of Yahweh and of Jesus. It is to make it possible for individuals and nations to live free from oppression in conditions of liberty and justice and with the chance to develop their potentials to the full. This understanding of mission would give us Christians the possibility of cooperating with a religious group which promotes the kingdom in the economic, political, cultural and religious arenas. And at the same time it would give the chance to influence the building of the kingdom according to the wishes of God, and the teachings and examples of Jesus.

Others prefer to speak of *God* as the content and focus of mission. The Word became human to complete God's revelation to humanity, to gather around God all nations and peoples. In this way all those who believe in God can dialogue together to enrich one another, to deepen their incomplete notions of that God, and to work together so that God will be "all in all," thus promoting the building of God's kingdom on earth.

There are others who prefer to speak of *establishing the church* as the essence of mission. People who believe that "establishing the church" is the proper object of mission see in the church instituted by Jesus all the means for the development of the kingdom. The church is seen as the beginning of the kingdom, the sacrament of the kingdom, and the instrument for its fulfillment—Noah's ark offering total and comprehensive salvation. And so, to spread the church is to spread the kingdom. To improve the church is to promote the best conditions for the advancement of the kingdom (Pro Mundi Vita 1984).

Finally, others prefer to speak of *life* as the essence of mission. God, who is life, has chosen to share life with the universe and, to a deeper degree, with intelligent beings. Jesus, the son of God, is viewed as the fullness of life come to earth to bring life in abundance and to redeem and renew this life for all creatures through his death and resurrection. The kingdom inaugurated by him embraces life in all its manifestations, and does away with all that impedes life and its growth according to the potential of each creature. Those who do not enjoy the fullness of life, or are impeded from doing so on account of external or internal factors, personal or imposed by others, are the focus of special consideration and love from God and Jesus. It is to them that God offers love and support against those who abuse the poor and do not allow them to enjoy the fullness of life in all its manifestations. The Church is then seen as God's means for promoting and enhancing life.

It is evident that each of these models contains elements that are candidates for the status of core content elements for mission. But if we compare them with the essence of Mary's mission, they will be seen to lack what I consider to be the most relevant, and probably the unique element of her mission—*making visible and palpable all that God is and all that God wills for humanity*. The angel of the annunciation began the formulation of this mission:

You are to conceive and bear a son, and you must name him Jesus. He will be great, and will be called Son of the Most High. The Lord God will give him the throne of his ancestor David: he will rule over the house of Jacob for ever, and his reign will have no end (Lk. 1:31-33).

At the stable of Bethlehem, the angels added other elements to this description—"Do not be afraid. Listen. I bring you news of great joy, a joy to be shared by the whole world. Today, in the town of David, a savior has been born: he is Christ the Lord" (Lk. 2:10-11). Simeon then said:

My eyes have seen your salvation, which you have prepared in sight of all the peoples, a light of revelation to the Gentiles, and glory for your People Israel ... Behold this child is destined for the fall and rise of many in Israel, and to be a sign that will be contradicted (Lk. 2:30-31, 34).

It seems to me that the essence of Mary's mission is well described in the above verses of the gospel. Mary has agreed to bear, to raise, and to accompany all the way to Calvary a son who was the sacrament of God on earth and who was to fulfil all the promises made to Israel as the prototype of all humanity. And so, by fulfilling all these promises made to Israel, he extended them to all peoples and to the whole of creation (R.M. 4-5). If we try to analyze all the elements of Mary's mission contained in the above quotes in the light of God's design contained in the Old and New Testaments, we may be able to see the core and the complexity of Mary's mission, and I hope we can then relate it to our times.

The son to whom Mary agreed to give birth is the Word of God. John testifies to this in a unique way—"In the beginning was the Word, the Word was with God, and the Word was God" (Jn. 1:1). "Through him all things came to be, not one thing had its being but through him" (Jn. 1:3). "The Word was made flesh, he lived among us" (Jn. 1:14). The son of Mary— who is the Word of God—has touched all creatures and has influenced all that exists. He has left the imprint of his being on every creature. The Word belongs to God and to the world. The Word is the inner principle of all peoples. All that exists, all that God has made, bears the indelible imprint of the Word. Every nation and all the peoples of the earth have been continually under the creating and vivifying influence of the Word. What a lesson in humility and what great joy this consideration holds for missionaries. The Word of God is waiting for them wherever they go. Everything is sacred in its core.

In Mary the Word became like unto us creatures. Its historical existence, its actions as a human being, the mystery of life, death, and resurrection are the gift of Mary to all who are called by the Spirit to recognize in Jesus the Word of God. This historical announcement of the Word of God— accepted through the revealing light of the Spirit—is the great treasure known to the followers of Jesus. Only they can say in the power of the Spirit—"You are the Messiah" (Mk. 8:29). It is true that the redemptive action of the incarnate Word touches the whole of creation, redeems all creatures, and brings new renewed life to the whole cosmos. Nevertheless, the awareness of this mystery and the acceptance of this event are entrusted to Christians. This consideration entails consequences for all Christians, especially those "in mission."

In mission we are the announcers of this good news. The Spirit in the other key dimension of mission reveals this to the inner heart of human beings mysteriously. The missionary announces it, or as Pope John Paul II says, "to propose" (R.M. 39) it to as many as possible. The Spirit works in human hearts.

To know what God has done in Jesus is a source of great consolation. It becomes a strong motivation for the development of our relationship with God and as missioners. Intelligent beings act under the influence of knowledge. We Christians have as an unmerited gift to know the plan of God in the Word made flesh. To us, then, is open a possibility to form a personal relationship with God and the Word. And with our mission we are given a chance to offer to others the opportunity to come to the same awareness, knowing full well that only the Spirit can open their minds to know and move their will to accept the mystery we announce to them. This realization will keep us humble as Mary was, because it is the Spirit who helps bring Christ to birth in the minds of people. We are only the heralds of the mystery.

This historical Jesus, whom we know and accept as the Word of God, is not totally ours or only ours. He also belongs to those who do not know him explicitly in the power of the Spirit. Mary understood this truth in the temple when she was asked by her son: "Why were you looking for me? Did you not know that I must be busy with my Father's affairs?" (Lk. 2:49). Mary gives birth to a being who existed before her, feeds an infant who does not belong to her completely, and loves the fruit of her womb, whose nature and essence constitute a mystery also for her. Jesus is hers—but not absolutely. She sees him—but she does not fully understand him. She admires him—even when he does not seem to care or notice her.

We missionaries find ourselves in the same situation. If we are not able to be like Mary in our work for Jesus, if we are not open to the surprises which God has in store for us, we will be confused by his presence where we least expect it. His ways are not always in conformity with juridical, theological, and ecclesial canons. Like Mary, it should be enough to know Jesus in the Spirit. We should be happy to have the opportunity to announce him to the nations but we should also be ready to be surprised by him and to discover him in surprising ways and moments.

This historical Jesus, who lived a life completely under the influence of the Spirit and who suffered a terrible death, was raised from the dead and has been declared by the Father to be Lord of creation and of history. In him, as human person and divine Word, all creation is summed up, the earlier covenant renewed and a new one begun. That covenant is being completed in history's surprises. Jesus, the Christ, we believe to be the center of the universe, the Lord of creation, the savior, the redeemer of all, the kingdom in all its fullness, and in all its characteristics both human and divine (R.M. 16-18). In preaching this Jesus, the Christ, one preaches the kingdom, promotes its qualities, and offers life in all its fullness (Eph. 1:3-14). Also, this Christ is the head of the church (Eph. 1:23), the community of his followers.

This short exposition of Jesus the Christ as the essence of Christian mission would not be complete unless mention is made of the fact that he lives among the poor in a very particular way (Mt. 25:31-40). And this makes the poor the most effective and concrete sign of his presence in the world. The poor become the call for justice, for continued efforts at building the kingdom, for providing a full and peaceful life for all. The poor are the voice inviting us to correct what is evil, to promote what is just, to complete what is imperfect, and to cure what is sick. The poor are the conscience of God for society, the justice of God for the oppressed, the judgment of God for oppressors, and the hope of God for the marginalized and ostracized people of society.

Mary's mission was centered around the gift of a son who is totally human and divine, the savior of all, the center of creation, life for all, the head of the new creation and of the new community, the Lord of history and of all progress, judgment against all injustices and all perpetrators of iniquity, and the apex of all reality. It seems to me that all those involved in mission would do well to identify the essence of their mission with that of Mary—as a sign of fidelity to the dynamics of the gospel and as an exigency to manifest the universality of the gospel message.

At this point I must discuss, however briefly, an objection which is raised by those who promote mission as life, church, kingdom and God. They sometimes state that in a pluralistic world divided by religious diversity presenting the essence of mission as a proclamation centered on the person of Jesus as the Christ will deepen the divisions within humankind and hinder the efforts of world religions to collaborate for the good of humanity. On the contrary, they state, if "God," the "kingdom," or "life" become the center of mission, then all religions could have the same focus and the same purpose. Then the dialogue between religious communities will become simpler and working together easier. This objection raises immensely important questions.

I firmly believe that if we Christians present Jesus Christ as I have tried to describe him, our mission would become a source of dialogue and motivation for cooperation with other religions, and indeed with the humanistic movements in our society. To present Jesus as the Word of God who is present and operative in each people, who animates progress, who is imprinted in the cultural and religious expressions of peoples, written about by the various sacred books, would be to present him as a bridge and not a chasm between religions and humanistic movements. To present Jesus as the cosmic Christ of whom Paul speaks—whose redemptive act has influence on all, who leads all toward the God of love and life, who consecrates in himself all that exists, who moves creation towards the kingdom, and humanity towards becoming God's family on earth—is to join with all those who put God at the center of life and history. Doing so is to focus on the kingdom, to highlight the fullness of life, and to look for points of unity in the diversity of cultural and religious expressions. To announce the Word made flesh, who lived the same kind of life we do, who experienced human tragedy and an ignominious death followed by victory is an enrichment for the whole human family, an example for all to imitate, and the strongest hope for the poor, the persecuted, is to make present a source of joy for the whole of humanity.

The son of Mary, even for those who understand him only as a human being or another religious leader (as he was for Gandhi and many other outstanding religious leaders of our times) is a precious gift who inspires deep religious feelings, constructive actions, and motivation for radical socio-cultural changes. The son of Mary, as the Word of God, is echoed in all religions and cultures inasmuch as they are expressions of God's presence and influence on all peoples. The cultural and religious manifestations of the peoples are not only *not* rejected or condemned in such a view of Jesus, but they take on meaning as an integral part of the activity of the Word of God, and thus they are judged to be fundamentally good even when they need completion and correction. The son of Mary, as the risen Christ and the Lord of creation, not only does not deny anything to the present life, to human progress, to the future of humanity, to the hope of humanity, or to the needs of justice for the poor, but is the inner and dynamic force of progress, a pledge of the certainty of victory over evil, a consolation and an example for all humans, and the inspiration for those who fight for a better future and a more just society.

It is clear that in the past mission often seemed to offer this Jesus within a Western context which automatically excluded any other cultural and religious values. The message was sometimes framed in a theological framework so narrow that it made Jesus a cause of division rather than unity. He came to be viewed as a figure who authorized a Western Christian superiority complex and who condemned other forms of religious experience. His main concern was portrayed as the afterlife rather than this life. To the extent this occurred, however, we were presenting some other Jesus than the one whom Mary gave to the world!

I have had many occasions to attend meetings of religious groups and of humanistic movements in many parts of the world. I never perceived great resistance to the presentation of Jesus that I described above. Moreover, the people I met often were begging us Christians to speak plainly about our faith. They wanted to know this Jesus, so that they could feel close to him. They would be ecstatic at the values and teachings of Jesus presented as I sketched them and could become highly motivated by Jesus and teaching about him.

CONCLUSION

The mission of the church is perennial in its substance but it is changeable in its formulation and external manifestations. The form it takes in diverse circumstances depends on the different historical moments and human situations in which it is proclaimed. In a world as pluralistic as we today know ours to be, the formulation of mission and its praxis are as varied as are the situations we encounter. The historical multiplicity of formulations of mission do not eliminate its essence or even obscure it.

By looking at Mary's mission, we may bring into better focus the essence of our own mission. For us the essence of mission, as it was for Mary, is to announce and offer Jesus the Christ in all his fullness and richness. In him, as the Word of God and the son of Mary, other important aspects of mission—such as life, kingdom, God—can easily be developed. In fact, even those who state that kingdom, life, liberation, dialogue, or church are the essence of mission, indirectly point to Christ who is life, who announces, symbolizes and effects God's kingdom, who is the center of the dialogue between God and humans, and who is the promoter of justice through love and justice. Since the mission of Mary was one of manifesting bodily the Word of God, we missionaries can take inspiration from her mission, make it our own, and concretize it in the historical situations of the peoples with whom we live. This insight will make the Gospel our own consolation and a reason for those with whom we share the message throughout the world to hope for the salvation revealed in Jesus the Christ born of Mary.

BIBLIOGRAPHY

Amaladoss, Michael. "Culture and Dialogue," in *International Review of Mission.* Geneva: WCC, vol. 74, April 1985.

Anderson, Gerald H., and Thomas F. Stransky. *Christ's Lordship and Religious Pluralism.* Maryknoll, N.Y.: Orbis Books, 1981.

Appiah-Kubi, Kofi, and Sergio Torres, eds. *African Theology en Route.* Maryknoll, N.Y.: Orbis Books, 1979.

Araya, Victorio. *God of the Poor.* Maryknoll, N.Y.: Orbis Books, 1987.

Balasuriya, Tissa. *Planetary Theology.* Maryknoll, N.Y.: Orbis Books, 1984.

Bellagamba, Anthony. "Preferential Option for the Poor," *African Christian Studies* 3 (No. 3, 1987): 19-48.

————. "The Church of the Future," *African Christian Studies* 6 (No. 3, 1990): 54-72.

Bennett, Anne McGrew. *From Woman-Pain to Woman-Vision.* Minneapolis: Fortress, 1989.

Beti, Mongo. *The Poor Christ of Bomba.* London: Heinemann, 1983.

Blau, Johannes. *The Missionary Nature of the Church.* New York: McGraw Hill, 1962.

Boff, Leonardo. *Unexpected News.* Philadelphia: Westminster, 1984.

————. *Church: Charism and Power.* London: SCM Press, 1985.

————. *Ecclesiogenesis: The Base Communities Reinvent the Church.* Maryknoll, N.Y.: Orbis Books, 1986.

Briggs, K. C., and I. B. Meyers. *Meyers-Briggs Type Indicator.* Palo Alto, Calif.: Consulting Psychologists Press, 1986.

Brown, Raymond E. *Biblical Reflections on Crises Facing the Church.* New York: Paulist Press, 1975.

Brown, Robert McAfee. *Gustavo Gutiérrez: An Introduction to Liberation Theology.* Maryknoll, N.Y.: Orbis Books, 1990.

Buber, Martin. *I and Thou.* Edinburgh: T & T Clark, 1984.

Bühlmann, Walbert. *The Coming of the Third Church.* Maryknoll, N.Y.: Orbis Books, 1977.

————. *God's Chosen Peoples.* Maryknoll, N.Y.: Orbis Books, 1982.

————. *The Church of the Future.* Maryknoll, N.Y.: Orbis Books, 1986.

————. *With Eyes to See.* Maryknoll, N.Y.: Orbis Books, 1990.

Byrne, Lavinia. *Women Before God: Our Own Spirituality.* Mystic, Connecticut: Twenty-Third Publications, 1988.

Cabestrero, Teofilo. *Ministers of God, Ministers of the People.* Maryknoll, N.Y.: Orbis Books, 1982.

Calian, C. S. *Today's Pastor in Tomorrow's Church.* Philadelphia: Westminster, 1982.

Camps, Arnulf. *Partners in Dialogue: Christianity and Other Religions.* Maryknoll, N.Y.: Orbis Books, 1983.

Castillejo, Irene Claremont de. *Knowing Woman: A Feminine Psychology.* New York: Harper & Row, 1973.

Catholic Higher Institute of East Africa (CHIEA). *Programme of Studies: 1989-1990.* Nairobi, 1989.

Césaire, Aime. *Discourse on Colonialism.* New York: Monthly Press, 1972.

Clark, David. *The Liberation of the Church.* Selly Oak, U.K.: National Center for Christian Communities and Network, 1989.

Clarke, Thomas E. "To Make Peace, Evangelize Culture," *America* (June 2, 1984): 413-17.

Cleary, Edward L. *Crisis and Challenge: The Church in Latin America.* Maryknoll, N.Y.: Orbis Books, 1985.

Clinebell, N. *Basic Types of Pastoral Care and Counseling.* Nashville: Abingdon, 1984.

Cobb, John B., Jr. *Christ in a Pluralistic Age.* Philadelphia, Westminster, 1975.

Conn, Joann Wolski, ed. *Women's Spirituality: Resource for Christian Development.* New York: Paulist, 1986.

Cosmao, Vincent. *Challenging the World: An Agenda for the Churches.* Maryknoll, N.Y.: Orbis Books, 1984.

Cullmann, Oscar. *Jesus and the Revolutionaries.* New York: Harper & Row, 1970.

Degrijse, Omer. *Going Forth.* Maryknoll, N.Y.: Orbis Books, 1984.

Donnelly, Doddy. *Team — Theory and Practice of Team Ministry.* New York: Paulist Press, 1977.

Donovan, Vincent. *Christianity Rediscovered.* Maryknoll, N.Y.: Orbis Books, 1982.

Döpfner, Julius. *The Questioning Church.* Baltimore: Newman, 1964.

Dulles, Avery. *Models of the Church.* Garden City, N.Y.: Doubleday, 1974; Maryknoll, N.Y.: Orbis Books, 1992.

———. *The Resilient Church.* Dublin: Gill & McMillan, 1978.

———. *The Catholicity of the Church.* Oxford: Clarendon, 1985, 1987.

———. *The Survival of Catholicism.* New York: Harper & Row, 1988a.

———. *The Reshaping of Catholicism.* New York: Harper & Row, 1988b.

Ebousi Boulaga, F. *Christianity without Fetishes: An African Critique and Recapture of Christianity.* Maryknoll, N.Y.: Orbis Books, 1984.

Echegaray, Hugo. *The Practice of Jesus.* Maryknoll, N.Y.: Orbis Books, 1984.

Fabella, Virginia. *Asia's Struggle for Humanity: Towards a Relevant Theology.* Maryknoll, N.Y.: Orbis Books, 1980.

Fabella, Virginia, and Sergio Torres, eds. *Irruption of the Third World.* Maryknoll, N.Y.: Orbis Books, 1983.

———. *Doing Theology in a Divided World.* Maryknoll, N.Y.: Orbis Books, 1985.

Ferder, Fran, and John Heagle. *Partnership: Women and Men in Ministry.* Notre Dame: Ave Maria, 1989.

Feuillet, André. *The Priesthood of Christ and His Ministers.* Garden City, N.Y.: Doubleday, 1975.

Fiorenza, Elizabeth Schüssler. *In Memory of Her.* New York: Crossroad, 1983.

Fischer, Kathleen. *Women at the Well: Feminine Perspective on Spiritual Development.* New York: Paulist Press, 1988.

Gelpi, Donald. *Experiencing God.* New York: Paulist, 1978.

Gilligan, Carol. *In a Different Voice: Psychological Theory and Women's Development.* Cambridge: Harvard University Press, 1982.

Gorski, John. "Is World Mission Still Urgent Today?" *Omnis Terra* 22 (No. 187, 1988): 184-215.

Gray, Elizabeth Dodson, ed. *Sacred Dimensions of Women's Experience.* Wellesley, Mass.: Roundtable Press, 1988.

Gutiérrez, Gustavo. *On Job: God-Talk and the Suffering of the Innocent.* Maryknoll, N.Y.: Orbis Books, 1987.

———. *The Truth Shall Make You Free.* Maryknoll, N.Y.: Orbis Books, 1990.

Henriot, Peter, and Joseph Holland. *Social Analysis.* Maryknoll, N.Y.: Orbis Books, 1983.

Hickey, Raymond. *Modern Missionary Documents and Africa.* Dublin: Dominican Publications, 1982.

Holland, Joe. *Creative Communion.* New York: Paulist Press, 1989.

Keirsey, D., and M. Bates. *Please Understand Me: Character and Temperament Types*. Del Mar: Prometheus Nemesis Book Co., 1984.

King, Geoffrey. "Priests for the 21st Century," *East Asia Pastoral Review* 27 (No. 1, 1990): 86-101.

Knitter, Paul. *No Other Name? A Critical Survey of Christian Attitudes toward World Religions*. Maryknoll, N.Y.: Orbis Books, 1985.

Küng, Hans. *The Church*. New York: Sheed & Ward, 1967.

Laye, Camara. *The African Child*. Glasgow: Fontana/Collins, 1982.

Luzbetak, Louis. *The Church and Cultures*. Maryknoll, N.Y.: Orbis Books, 1989.

Maduro, Otto. "Notes for a South-North Dialogue in Mission from a Latin American Perspective," *Missiology* 15 (No. 2, 1987): 62-75.

Mbiti, John. *Introduction to African Religion*. London: Heinemann, 1975.

McBrien, Richard P. *Church: The Continuing Quest*. Baltimore: Newman, 1970.

————. *The Remaking of the Church*. New York: Harper & Row, 1973.

————. *Catholicism*. New York: Harper & Row, 1980; London: Geoffrey Chapman, 1984.

McDonagh, Enda, et al. *The Church in Mission*. London: Geoffrey Chapman, 1969.

McGavaran, Donald, ed. *Church Growth and Christian Mission*. New York: Harper & Row, 1965.

Meehan, Francis X. *A Contemporary Social Spirituality*. Maryknoll, N.Y.: Orbis Books, 1984.

Mejia, Rodrigo. *Seeking and Finding God in All Things*. Nairobi: St. Paul, 1986.

Metz, Johann B. *The Emergent Church*. London: SCM Press, 1981.

Mische, Gerald, and Patricia Mische. *Towards a Human World Order*. New York: Paulist Press, 1977.

Molari, Carlo. *La Fede e il suo Linguaggio*. Assisi: Cittadella Editrice, 1972.

Motte, Mary. *A Critical Examination of Mission Today*. Washington, D.C.: U.S. Catholic Mission Association, 1987.

Nacpil, E., and D. J. Elwood, eds. *The Human and the Holy: Asian Perspectives in Christian Theology*. Quezon City: New Day Publishers, 1978.

National Council of Catholic Bishops. *The Challenge of Peace: God's Promise and Our Response*. Washington: NCCB Publications, 1983.

————. *Catholic Social Teaching and the U.S. Economy*. Washington: NCCR Publications, 1986.

————. *Partners in the Mystery of Redemption*. Washington: NCCB Publications, 1988.

Neil, Stephen. *Call to Mission*. Philadelphia: Fortress, 1970.

Nouwen, Henri. *The Wounded Healer*. Garden City, N.Y.: Image Books, 1979.

————. *Intimacy*. New York: Harper & Row, 1981.

Nzekwu, Onuora. *Blade among the Boys*. London: Heinemann, 1978.

O'Halloran, James. *Signs of Hope: Developing Small Christian Communities*. Maryknoll, N.Y.: Orbis Books, 1991.

Osthathios, G. M. *Theology of a Classless Society*. Maryknoll, N.Y.: Orbis Books, 1980.

Paul VI. *Africae Terrarum*. 1967.

————. *Evangelii Nuntiandi*. 1975.

Pennington, Basil. *Centering Prayer*. Garden City, N.Y.: Doubleday, 1980.

Penoukou, Efoe J. *Eglises d'Afrique*. Paris: Editions Karthala, 1984.

Pico, Juan Hernandez, and Jon Sobrino. *Theology of Christian Solidarity*. Maryknoll, N.Y.: Orbis Books, 1985.

Pimenta, Simon I. "Intervention at the Synod of Reconciliation," *Osservatore Romano* (October 17, 1983).

Ponsi, Frank, I.M.C. "Attitudes of American Women Religious towards the Concept of Mission." Washington, D.C., n.d.

Power, David N. *Gifts that Differ: Lay Ministries Established and Unestablished*. New York: Pueblo, 1980.

Pro Mundi Vita. *John Paul II and the Mission of the Church Today*. Brussels, 1984.

Race, Allen. *Christian and Religious Pluralism.* London: SCM Press, 1983.

Raffle, Alveoli. *Worship Politics.* Maryknoll, N.Y.: Orbis Books, 1981.

Rahner, Karl, and Josef Ratzinger. *The Episcopate and the Primacy.* New York: Herder & Herder, 1963.

Rahner, Karl. *Bishops: Their Status and Function.* Baltimore: Challenge Book, 1965.

———. "Towards a Fundamental Theological Interpretation of Vatican II," *Theological Studies,* vol. 40, no. 4, December 1979a.

———. *The Spirit in the Church.* London: Burns & Oates, 1979b.

———. *Belief Today.* London: Sheed & Ward, 1980.

———. *Concern for the Church.* New York: Crossroad, 1981.

———. *Practice of Faith.* London: SCM, 1985.

Ratzinger, Joseph. "Primary, Episcopate and Apostolic Succession" in Karl Rahner and Joseph Ratzinger, eds. *The Episcopacy and the Primacy.* New York: Herder, 1963.

Retif, A. *La Missione: Elementi di Teolgia e Spiritualità Missionaria.* Turin: Edizioni Missioni Consolata, 1965.

Ross, Kinsler, ed. *Ministry by the People.* Geneva: WCC, 1983.

Ruether, Rosemary Radford. *Mary: The Feminine Face of the Church.* Philadelphia: Westminster, 1977.

Russell, Letty M. *Human Liberation in a Feminine Perspective—A Theology.* Philadelphia: Westminster, 1974.

Santa Ana, Julio de. *Towards a Church of the Poor.* Geneva: WCC, 1979.

Schillebeeckx, Edward. *Ministry.* New York: Crossroad, 1981.

———. *The Church with a Human Face.* London: SCM Press, 1985.

Schineller, Peter. *A Handbook of Inculturation.* New York: Paulist, 1990.

Schreiter, Robert J. *Constructing Local Theologies.* Maryknoll, N.Y.: Orbis Books, 1985.

Segundo, Juan Luis. *The Hidden Motives at Pastoral Action.* Maryknoll, N.Y.: Orbis Books, 1972.

Serbin, Ken. "Pastoral Agents Movement Fledging Black Awareness in Brazil," *National Catholic Reporter* (April 20, 1990).

Seumois, André. *Théologie Missionaire,* 5 vols. Rome: Editiones Urbanianae, 1973-1980.

Shorter, Aylward. *Toward a Theology of Inculturation.* Maryknoll, N.Y.: Orbis Books, 1988.

Sobrino, Jon. *The True Church and the Poor.* Maryknoll, N.Y.: Orbis Books, 1984.

———. *Spirituality of Liberation.* Maryknoll, N.Y.: Orbis Books, 1989.

Song, C. S. *Christian Mission in Reconstruction: An Asian Analysis.* Maryknoll, N.Y.: Orbis Books, 1977.

———. *Tell Us Our Names: Story Theology from an Asian Perspective.* Maryknoll, N.Y.: Orbis Books, 1984.

Voillaume, René. *Ou est votre Foi?* Paris: Cerf, 1971.

———. *Retraite à Beni-Abbes: Entretiens sur la Vie Religieuse.* Paris: Cerf, 1973.

———. *Faith and Contemplation.* London: Darton, Longman and Todd, 1974.

———. *The Need for Contemplation.* London: Darton, Longman and Todd, 1978.

Wakatama, Pius. *Independence of the Third World Church: An African Perspective on the Missionary World.* Downers Grove, Ill.: Inter-Varsity Press, 1976.

———. *The Need for Contemplation.*

Waliggo, John. *Inculturation: Its Meaning and Urgency.* Nairobi: St. Paul, 1986.

Weakland, Rembert G. "Taking up a Global Church Agenda," *National Catholic Reporter* (October 13, 1989).

Wengst, Klaus. *Pax Romana and the Peace of Jesus Christ.* London: SCM Press, 1987.

Zago, Marcello. *Dialogo ed Evangelizzazione in Chiesa Locale ed Inculturazzione nella Missione.* Bologna: EMI, 1987.